Pearl Harbor

G·K
Hall
&C͉o

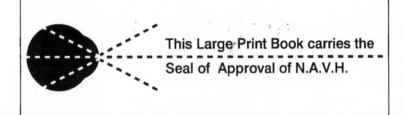

Pearl Harbor

Edwin P. Hoyt

G.K. Hall & Co. • Thorndike, Maine

Published in 2000 by arrangement with Wieser & Wieser, Inc.

G.K. Hall Large Print American History Series.

The text of this Large Print edition is unabridged.
Other aspects of the book may vary from the original edition.

Set in 16 pt. Plantin by Elena Picard.

Printed in the United States on permanent paper.

Library of Congress Cataloging-in-Publication Data

Hoyt, Edwin Palmer.
    Pearl Harbor / Edwin P. Hoyt.
      p. cm.
    Originally published: New York : Avon Books, 1991.
    Includes bibliographical references.
     ISBN 0-7838-9303-5 (lg. print : hc : alk. paper)
     1. Pearl Harbor (Hawaii), Attack on, 1941. I. Title.
D767.92 H69 2000
940.54′26—dc21   00-046550

Table of Contents

To Begin . . .

"Air Raid, Pearl Harbor, This Is Not a Drill. . . ."

December 7, 1941

As the hands of the clock swung around and passed midnight, and December 6 turned into December 7, the Japanese submarine *I-16* released the 20-foot midget submarine that it carried on its deck. An hour later, nine miles off the entrance to the Pearl Harbor channel, the *I-22* sent its two-man submarine on its way. The target: the ships inside Pearl Harbor, the big American naval base in the Hawaiian Islands, base of the U.S. Pacific Fleet, which was to be attacked today in the opening move of the Pacific war.

At 2:15 A.M. the *I-18*, which was sitting 12 miles off Pearl Harbor, let go her two-man midget submarine. Just before three o'clock the *I-20* launched its two-man midget, and half an hour later the *I-24* launched the fourth midget submarine.

As these events occurred in the hours of darkness of December 7, 200 miles to the north of Oahu Island the Japanese task force was nearing the point at which it would launch the aircraft that would attack the American fleet in conjunction with the midget torpedo attacks. The latter, of course, were to provide a diversion if possible. Admiral Isoroku Yamamoto, commander of the Japanese Combined Fleet and the father of the Pearl Harbor attack plan, regarded the midget submarine operation as sort of a stunt, but he could not deny that the midgets might have some value, and now was the time to test it.

Aboard the carriers, preflight operations had begun at midnight; the aircraft were being brought up from the hangar decks of the six carriers and spotted for takeoff.

A stream of messages from Tokyo brought all the information about affairs in Hawaii that the Naval General Staff could provide. Watchers had reported the arrival of ships of the Pacific Fleet after their week of defense exercises. Naval officers had contacted Hawaii by telephone in the afternoon of December 6 and reported that there was no sense of urgency on the island of Oahu.

By 5:00 A.M. all the pilots were up and dressed. Commander Mitsuo Fuchida, the leader of the air strike, ate breakfast and went to the briefing room underneath the flight deck to confer with the leaders of the torpedo bombers, dive-bombers, and fighter group that would accompany his twin-engined high-level bombers in the attack. The seas were roughing up and this would necessitate extreme caution in takeoff to prevent accidents.

After that conversation Commander Fuchida went aloft to the operations room of the flagship *Akagi* to report to Admiral Chuichi Nagumo, commander of the strike force, and his chief of staff Rear Admiral Ryunosuke Kusaka. He said the mission was ready to go and the admiral shook his hand and expressed confidence.

Then came the final briefing in which Commander Fuchida reviewed the attack plan. After that it was time for the pilots and aircrews to man their planes. The planes took off from the six carriers and formed up over the task force — high-level bombers at 10,000 feet, dive-bombers 1,000 feet higher, torpedo bombers at about 9,000 feet, all of them covered by the fast Zero fighters flying at 14,000 feet. When they were all in place, the high-level bombers took the lead and headed for the target:

PEARL HARBOR.

The leader of the air strike, Commander Fuchida, ordered the radio tuned in to Honolulu radio station KMBH, which would be their radio directional beam. And as they flew along toward the target, the clouds gathered below them at about 5,000 feet, effectively screening the Japanese attack force from prying eyes.

It was 7:00 A.M.

Three minutes later the American destroyer *Ward*, which was patrolling the entrance to Pearl Harbor that morning, established a sound contact on a submarine, and began dropping depth charges. Three minutes later a black oil bubble was sighted 300 yards astern of the destroyer.

Scratch one midget submarine.

At this moment a reconnaissance plane from the cruiser *Chikuma* was circling over Pearl Harbor and not attracting attention. The pilot was looking down to see nine battleships, one heavy cruiser, and six light cruisers. Meanwhile, a reconnaissance plane from the cruiser *Tone*, sent to Maui to examine the Lahaina anchorage, reported that the fleet was not in that area. The real object of that search was the three American aircraft carrier task forces, which were nowhere in evidence in the islands, much to the disappointment of the Japanese. So they knew that whatever elements of the American fleet were missing from Pearl Harbor — the carriers, in particular — were not in the Hawaiian Islands this day, but where were they? The absence of the camera and the inability of the Japanese to locate their areas of operations was to have a major effect on the Japanese air strike.

But at the moment, all attention was on the gamble that Admiral Nagumo considered to be desperate, the strike against Pearl Harbor.

At 7:33 Commander Fuchida's first wave of attack bombers reached a point 35 miles north of Oahu Island. Moments later, straining to see through his powerful binoculars, Commander Fuchida saw the gray-green mountains ahead of him, and as the aircraft drew near the island Fuchida picked up his rocket pistol and at 7:40

fired a signal flare. The attack was on.

Below, Commander Fuchida counted seven battleships, not the nine reported by the *Chikuma* pilot. Actually there were eight battlewagons, one of them, the *Pennsylvania*, in dry dock. One ship, the *Utah*, which the *Chikuma* pilot had thought was a battleship, was actually an old battleship now used as a target ship.

At 7:49 the Japanese aircraft were in position to attack. Commander Fuchida gave the signal to charge and the radioman began to send it. The message was picked up by a waiting radioman aboard the Japanese fleet at Hashirajima Harbor in the Inland Sea, a staff officer took the message to the chief of staff, and a few moments later Admiral Yamamoto knew that the event he had both hoped for and feared in recent months had come to pass. His airplanes were attacking the American fleet at Pearl Harbor.

At 7:55 on Ford Island, U.S. Navy Commander Logan Ramsay saw an airplane streak across the station, and prepared to report the incident as a breach of safety regulations — until he realized that the red he saw on the aircraft was not a squadron commander's insignia but a Japanese flag, and that the object he saw drop from the plane was not a black bag but a bomb.

Commander Ramsay ran to the radio room of the Ford Island command center and told the radiomen on duty to send a single message, in the clear, in plain English.

"Air raid, Pearl Harbor. This is not a drill. . . ."

Chapter 1

The Darkening Clouds

In Volume 1 of my series on the Pacific war (*The Triumph of Japan*), I dealt with the Japanese military aspects of the China war and preparations for the Pacific war in a military sense. But I did not deal with the basic causes of that war, which lie much deeper than the military and were, indeed, ingrained in the Japanese soul in the nineteenth century. To put as good a face on the Japanese position as possible, one could say that their major aim in Asia was to free Asians from the boot of the white man. This was true, but it is an oversimplification, and the motivations of the Japanese military were not nearly so pure as that as the record shows very clearly in the planning that went on in the 1930s, and the excesses and arrogance of the Japanese military in the war years.

So, although this book is the story of the Pearl Harbor attack, in order to understand what happened and why, one must understand the Japanese, not only the military oligarchy that seized control in the 1930s, but the other side as well. The other side is epitomized by the man who planned and ordered the Pearl Harbor attack — Admiral Isoroku Yamamoto — who was opposed to warring on the United States and Britain and never believed that Japan could win such a war.

One must also understand that right or wrong, there were in the 1930s in Japan many people who truly believed that the Western powers were intent on encircling and strangling Japan and preventing her from becoming the leading world power that she believed herself capable of being and ready to be. One must also understand a streak of submissiveness and inferiority that runs through the Japanese character and is often expressed by apparent arrogance. There is also, as is common in Asia, an element of fatalism, expressed in the Buddhist philosophy as the wheel of life to which men are bound throughout their existence until they can achieve enlightenment, which frees them from the yoke of Karma. It was that streak of fatalism that caused the military leaders of Japan to opt for the uncertainty of war in 1941, full knowing that they did not have the resources to defeat the Western world in the long run, and that their only chance of any sort of victory (they said survival) was to reap the whirlwind, and then in the flush of victory to persuade the West to accept their conquests.

For a short time, between the 1940 signing of the Tripartite Pact that bound Japan, Germany,

14

and Italy as allies, the Japanese hoped that the Germans would win the war. But by the autumn of 1941, when Hitler was mired down in Russia and had failed to bring Britain down either by fierce bombardment or by the submarine campaign against shipping, it was apparent to the Japanese military leaders that they took a great risk in going to war. Their reasoning, aside from the juggernaut effect their actions had brought on them, or perhaps in justification of it, was that time was not on their side, and that each succeeding month would make the Japanese position less tenable. And meanwhile the oil and other resources were running out. One does not have to accept these conclusions to understand them and how they prompted the Japanese military to do what it did in those fateful months of November and December 1941.

Therefore in setting the stage for Pearl Harbor, I will explore in this volume the reasons for the behavior of the Japanese that led to the event.

After the China-Japan war began in the summer of 1937 the relationships between Japan and the Western world deteriorated steadily. It was inevitable that this should be so, because the Japanese had embarked on a course that could not but lead to eventual conflict with the European powers and the United States. The epitome of the course of action was the Japanese slogan of the late 1930s: Asia for the Asiatics.

The slogan represented policy that had been

the essential Japanese attitude since the 1850s, when Japan was forcibly opened to Western trade and influence by the black ship fleet of Commodore Matthew Perry. In those days wise Japanese saw that there was no effective way of keeping the white man out of Asia. If Japan did not want to be swallowed, as had been India, the Philippines, the East Indies, and Southeast Asia, then Japan would have to pretend to accept the white man, learn his ways, and when the time was ripe, eject him from Asia.

So the Japanese learned to make gunpowder and guns and modern ships. Under the Meiji Emperor, whose Imperial power was wrested from the shoguns who had ruled Japan for six hundred years, the Japanese became assiduous students of the Industrial Revolution. They saw the need for a modern defense force and created an army on the model of the Prussian, which they admired in Europe, and a navy on the model of the British Royal Navy. Foreign companies were eager to come and trade in Japan. They established factories and industries, but the Japanese were wise, and although they took from the foreigners, and paid for what they took, they did not allow the foreigners to dominate their emergence into a modern society. The foreigners were encouraged to come and teach the Japanese, and when the Japanese had learned, they ejected the foreign companies that had taught them.

One of the prices of dealing with foreigners, from the Asian point of view, was the demand by the Westerners that they be tried in their own courts for crimes and that they have other special privileges. Extraterritorialism, they called it. It was an accompaniment of colonialism, a recognition by the government that granted it of the superiority of the whites over the Asians.

When the white men came to Japan, of course, they demanded extraterritoriality, and to achieve other aims they wished to pursue, the Japanese granted it. But by 1882, the Japanese had achieved much of their program of modernization, bringing Japan into the nineteenth century industrially.

Japan had three major shipyards capable of building warships, fifty-one modern merchant ships flying her flag, fifty-two factories using modern methods of production, ten mines, seventy-five miles of railroad, and a telegraph system that extended around the nation. Five years later all this had increased manyfold, the modern army and reserve totaled nearly 300,000 men, and the navy was building twenty-three modern warships. The Meiji government had decided on a policy like that of the European and American nations: Japan would become an empire with her own colonies. She would not be colonized. In 1890 Japan already had a colony, the Ryukyu Islands, which included Okinawa and the Kuriles, which were useful for fishing and naval bases and not much else. Japan coveted other territory: the big island of Taiwan, which was Chinese territory: Hainan, another virtually undeveloped Chinese island;

and Korea, which for hundreds of years had been a Chinese vassal kingdom. The European nations were doing their best to rip off segments of Chinese territory, and the Japanese government decided to do the same. They knew that in Korea, and in Manchuria, which they also coveted, they would be challenging the Russians, who wanted both territories.

The period 1889 to 1894 was marked by enormous ferment in Japan, much of it centering around Japan's relations with the Western world. Extraterritoriality had been granted but the Japanese people had loathed it for many years, and cabinets had resigned over the issue when they failed to meet the demand to end what the general Japanese public regarded as a disgraceful system. After a shrewd assessment of the realities of Asia, Britain led the way in relinquishing extraterritoriality. It was not done from any benevolence, however, but because the British saw the handwriting on the wall. By this time the Meiji government had become an outright oligarchy to counteract the restlessness of the public, and for the foreigners, it was either conform to the Japanese way of doing things or get out. Britain chose to try to preserve her business interests in Japan by ending extraterritoriality, and it was not long before the other nations had to follow suit. So by the 1890s Japan had achieved a position in Asia unmatched by any other Asian nation. She was totally independent and regarded herself as the equal — at least — of all the European nations. Her government did not trumpet the fact, but the intention of Japan was fixed: to achieve leadership of Asia and drive the white man out altogether.

In the Japanese view, the key to all this development lay in China, that great rotting empire that covered so much of the Asian continent. And it was to China that she turned, first to rip off her own share of colonial power in Taiwan, later in Shandong, Manchuria, and North China, and later — 1937 — to fuse around China the idea of an Asian coalition led by Japan, the Greater East Asia Co-Prosperity Sphere. The name developed only after 1941, and the whole concept was regarded by the Western Allies as nothing but a ploy to help Japan in World War II. But this denigration of the idea misses the whole point of the Japanese endeavor. Certainly Japan intended to be first among Asian nations. Certainly she intended to have her way in Asia. But the Japanese saw nothing in this attitude that would preclude the independence of the various countries involved — so long as they stayed within the Japanese structure for Asia. Indeed, from the beginning of the Pacific conflict, the Japanese had incipient plans, at least, to give independence to the Philippines, the Dutch East Indies, and Indochina.

Chapter 2

Roots of Conflict

One country does not attack another without reason, even if the reason is not readily apparent to the neighboring countries and the world. And the reasons for the Japanese attack on Pearl Harbor can be found in events that began in 1905. That was the year of the Treaty of Portsmouth, which ended the Russo-Japanese War.

Before 1905, Japan's perceived enemy was Czarist Russia. To be sure, the Japanese had attacked China and fought in Korea, but this was a part of the Japanese expansionist programs, and the Japanese never considered China as an enemy. Nor did the Japanese in the nineteenth century consider the United States to be a potential enemy. Very shortly after the opening of Japan, American ambitions for trade and territory were submerged in a suicidal civil war, which left no energy or resources to waste on the outside world.

When the Civil War ended, and America again turned outward, one of its early acts was to bring Japanese cadets to the U.S. Naval Academy in Annapolis. The atmosphere between the two countries was idyllic.

When America did begin to show signs of territorial ambition in the Pacific, in the 1880s, her attention was turned to the South Pacific to Hawaii and China, but not to Japan. The first irritations began when the Chinese came to America and proved so successful as workers that the Irish (who did most of the manual labor at that time) became frightened and then enraged, and secured passage of laws limiting the immigration of the Chinese. This was quickly extended to the Japanese as they became a perceived threat to West Coast farmers because of their frugality and efficiency. The Chinese Exclusion Acts and the "Gentleman's Agreement" with Japan to limit Japanese immigration to the United States left scars, which were more lasting because the acts were accompanied by open racism that soon had most Americans believing they were superior to the people of Asia by some great gift of birth. Almost precisely the same pattern was followed in Australia as well. By the beginning of the twentieth century the view was that the Japanese were the "Yellow Peril" who somehow threatened the well-being of the West.

The year 1905 marked a turning point for the worse in Japanese-American relations. This was the year in which President Theodore Roosevelt, offering his "good offices" to bring an end to the Russo-Japanese War, sided with the Russians to prevent the Japanese from securing a cash payment in reparations for a war the Japanese had started. If that seemed fair to the world, it enraged the Japanese officer class of the army and navy, because they had been counting on cash to restore the Japanese budget trim and guarantee military expansion. Instead, the virtually bankrupt Japanese government had to trim all its sails sharply, and the blow fell very hard on the military. It was at this juncture that the Japanese first officially perceived the United States as their enemy, and it was indicated in the Japanese naval war plan, which envisaged a struggle with America for the control of the Pacific.

The first saber rattling in this growing conflict was American. Concerned about the Japanese capability in the Pacific, Roosevelt sought expert advice and was assured that the Japanese would be years in recovering their military strength from the ravage of the war with the Russians. But the fact — which he soon learned — was that the Japanese were continuing to build their power, and particularly their naval strength. To impress the Japanese primarily, Roosevelt decided to send the American fleet around the world in a show of strength. Actually its strength was quite limited — Admiral Robley D. Evans could muster only sixteen major warships, many of them ill-equipped and undermanned. Newspapers and loud talkers of both countries spoke openly of war. And for what real reason? There was none; the talk stemmed from irresponsible journalism, and from super-patriotism and race hatred in both countries. So the Great White American Fleet sailed around the world on a goodwill mission and ended up stirring ill will in Japan that would last for forty years.

World War I tended to erode some of the scars that had built up when the Japanese and Americans found themselves on the same side, fighting Germany. Japan was first to do so, entering gladly under the terms of the Anglo-Japanese alliance, for the war gave the Japanese a chance to seize from Germany the Chinese colony of Kiaochao, in Shandong Province. Americans and Japanese later shared a wary vigil in Siberia, trying to police the railway, ostensibly to allow the Czech Legion of Habsburg Empire war prisoners to make their way around the world to fight for the Allied cause. But the occupation became political and mired in the tangle of the Russian civil war of 1919.

Tempers frayed more in the next few years as the Japanese sought naval parity with the United States and Britain and were refused time and again. This refusal was a great blow to Japanese pride, for the Japanese considered themselves to be the natural policeman of Asia and this role was denied to them in the Washington Naval Conference of 1921, and again in the London Conferences of 1930 and 1934. It was after the failure of the Conference of 1934 that Japan embarked on a secret naval building program in defiance of the world. By this time, of course, Japan was an outlaw, branded as an aggressor in her seizure of Manchuria and creation of the puppet state of Manchukuo, whose government was subject to the Japanese Army.

But the insurmountable difficulty between Japan and the United States arose in the 1920s and continued. The source of the quarrel was the status of China.

Both America and Japan laid claim to having special relationships with China. The Japanese interest was far older. Chinese priests had brought the Buddhist religion to Japan just after the first millennium of what was known as the Christian era. The Japanese had borrowed the Chinese writing system. Chinese literature pervaded Japanese classical studies. The Japanese had stoutly resisted Chinese efforts to colonize their country and had turned back two invasions by Kublai Khan in the fourteenth century. In the twentieth century, Sun Yat-sen, the founder of the Chinese Republic, had sought sanctuary, finance, and a wife in Japan. Chiang Kai-shek, his heir, had learned military science in Japan. The Japanese of the twentieth century envisioned an Asian federation, led by Japan and supported by the enormous human and physical resources of China.

The Western powers, particularly Britain and America, resisted in every way the Japanese desire to take over the management of Chinese political affairs and Japanese encroachment into the business community. America, which had no territorial designs on China, particularly after the disastrous Philippines experiment, insisted on what it called the "Open Door" policy, which gave equal treatment to American business in comparison with any others. This was not the Japanese way of doing business; the Japanese preferred monopolies and cartels.

These interests should have collided at the time of the Manchurian takeover, but the Americans and British were so preoccupied with their economic problems that they did not resist Japanese expansionism at the time that they could have stopped it.

The confrontations began to come in the middle 1930s in Shanghai, on the Yangtze River, and in North China, as the Japanese advanced and pursued their claims. When the incident at Marco Polo Bridge was magnified into a war by Japanese Army ambition, the conflict intensified. Tension increased in such international centers as Shanghai, as the Japanese military and naval presence increased. The fighting along the Yangtze River reached Nanking in December 1937, and shortly before that capital city of China fell to the Japanese, the *Panay* incident brought Japanese-American tensions to a new high. On December 11, the day before the city fell, Japanese Navy aircraft from the carriers and from airfields near Shanghai set out to support the Japanese army advance by destroying Chinese vessels on the central Yangtze. In fact, without discrimination they attacked everything they saw, and the vessels included three tankers of the Standard Oil Company, the American gunboat *Panay*, and four British gunboats. Japanese Army artillery also attacked the British gunboats. The result was that the three American tankers and the *Panay* were sunk, a matter that could have brought the United States to attack Japan and declare war at that moment. The incident was smoothed over because Admiral Isoroku Yamamoto, the deputy navy minister, was truly appalled by the lengths to which his navy had gone and managed to persuade Ambassador Joseph Grew of his sincerity. But more important, the U.S. government was not then ready to go to war, and the American public was much less so.

The general mobilization of Japanese society in 1938 gave a clue to which way the wind was blowing. Japan that year declared the Chinese government of Chiang Kai-shek to be persona non grata, and began dealing with a puppet group established in Nanking with Japanese assistance, the government of Wang Ching-wei, a dissident leader of the Kuomintang political party and once chief political assistant to Sun Yat-sen. The idea was to try to swing Chinese sentiment behind Wang's government, but it failed miserably. Chiang Kai-shek moved his government to Chongqing on the Yangtze River in Szechuan Province and continued to resist the Japanese.

The Imperial Army had completely miscalculated the strength of resistance of the Chinese and the determination of the Western powers, particularly the United States, to prevent the Japanese conquest of China. And by 1938 conquest was what it had become. Originally the Japanese army believed that Chiang could be forced to accept a pro-Japanese policy, but by 1938 it was apparent that this would not come about. Japan was then faced with the problem of consolidating gains and standing still or pursuing the conquest. The militarists, not yet understanding the depth of their inability to conquer, plunged blindly ahead. Their aim now was to cut Chiang's lifelines to the West, which would mean the end of military and even food supplies. The lifelines ran through Indochina, up to Hanoi, and then up the Red River valley and to Kunming and thence to Chongqing, and to Kunming over the Burma road, up the Irrawaddy River from Rangoon to Lashio and then by truck over the Himalayas.

The American response to this effort was to announce in the summer of 1939 the American intention to terminate its trade treaty with Japan, which was the precursor to cutting off Japanese supplies of oil and steel.

By June 1940 the Japanese had put such pressure on the British that they closed the Burma road to Chinese traffic. France was just collapsing and the British were faced with possible invasion by the Germans. They had no time or energy for an Asian confrontation.

In the summer of 1940, the Germans and the Italians were allied in their war against Britain and the Italians belatedly tried to cash in on the fall of

France. They failed in that attempt. More important about the alliance, the Japanese government saw in it a chance to intimidate the United States by bringing to the fore Japanese alliance with Germany and Italy, which could be called into play against the United States. And that is the basis on which the Tripartite Rome-Berlin-Tokyo Alliance was formed. Japanese Foreign Minister Yosuke Matsuoka said as much to the Russians, and so did Germany's foreign minister. Japan's basic concern was lest the United States intervene to stop Japanese attempts to conquer Chiang's China.

The Americans had not been pleased with the British decision to close down the Burma road and had pressed them to reopen. This came about just at the time that the Japanese thought they had closed down all Chiang Kai-shek's avenues to the outside world. In September 1940 the Japanese wrung from the supine French a concession to allow them to move their troops into Indochina and through there to attack the Chinese. Effectively then, this closed the ports of Indochina to the Chinese too. Britain's reaction to all this was to reopen the Burma road, and this is one of the reasons that the Japanese army began then to prepare for war against the West. It was not only the China question, but also the need to achieve raw materials supplies. The American reaction to the march into Indochina was to accelerate the closure of American markets, to cut off oil supplies, rubber, and steel. Without these essentials the

Japanese war machine would come to a stop, and since Japan had ambitions to seize Siberia and Mongolia, it was necessary that the war machine be kept in good shape. Thus the Japanese turned south and began negotiation with the Dutch (whose central government had also been overrun by the Germans) for concessions in the Dutch East Indies. If they did not get what they wanted, it was quite clear to all concerned, they would take it.

On September 27, 1940, Japan, Germany, and Italy signed the Tripartite Pact, which was the warning to America. At home in Japan this was the signal that the drive to free Asia from the white man's yoke had now reached a critical stage. That year it became clear inside the Japanese defense establishment that no matter how many people like Admiral Isoroku Yamamoto opposed war with the West, "those idiots" of the Imperial Army, who had achieved such tight control of the Japanese government that even Emperor Hirohito was afraid to face them down, were bent on war. That being so, in the fall of 1940, Admiral Yamamoto reached back in his memory of the Russo-Japanese War and decided on a plan of battle against the West.

The first trigger that sent new thoughts into Yamamoto's mind was the announcement that the United States had split its fleet into Atlantic and Pacific units. The second was the announcement that the Pacific Fleet would be moved from San Diego to Hawaii.

The Japanese battle plan had envisaged a fight against the American fleet, but in this manner: It was to be lured to Japanese waters to attack the Japanese fleet. En route it would be harried by Japanese submarines, which had long range and the most powerful and effective torpedoes in the world. Then somewhere, perhaps in the East China Sea, the American fleet would be engaged by the Japanese fleet with its superior battleships and cruisers, and the American fleet would be sent to the bottom of the sea. To make plans for such an eventuality was the task of Admiral Yamamoto. This was his responsibility as commander of the Combined Fleet, no matter how he felt about the issues personally. And the plan Yamamoto envisaged embodied his knowledge of the American military and their attitudes. He planned a surprise attack in the fashion of Admiral Heihachiro Togo against the Russians. Only thus, by defeating the American fleet and making it impossible for them to interfere, could the plan for the invasion of Southeast Asia succeed. Further, Yamamoto hoped that by defeating the American fleet Japan would play into the hands of the America Firsters (isolationists) and the pacifists in America, who were very strong. If that could happen then Americans could be kept at bay and a reasonable peace established, which would enable the Japanese to take over the resources they needed in Malaya and the Dutch East Indies, and thus shore up their military machine for continuation of the war in China to a successful end. At that point Japan would emerge as the leader of an Asian bloc that would no longer permit colonialism of any sort to exist in Asia. Japan then would be quite content to live with the West, so long as she controlled the East.

When Admiral Yamamoto brought forth his basic plan for a preemptive strike against the American fleet, the idea was loudly opposed by almost the entire Japanese naval establishment. It was not that the admirals disapproved of Yamamoto's strategy, to take on the American fleet and destroy it in the beginning. It was the Yamamoto method that they did not like. He wanted to use most of Japan's aircraft carriers for one major blow from the air at the Pacific Hawaii anchorage. The admirals could understand the concept. Many of them favored a plan to entice the American fleet to Japanese waters, whereupon the battleships would go forth and destroy the American battleships, which were much older and had smaller guns and less speed. Indeed, at this stage of the century a modern Japanese cruiser was more than a match for one of the American battleships. But to use aircraft carriers for this task seemed to be an ultimately foolish move. As everyone in Japan and every naval officer in the world knew, the aircraft carrier was a singular instrument of war. It carried powerful torpedoes and bombs that could be delivered by aircraft. But with its aircraft aloft, the carrier was virtually helpless except against air attack, from which it was protected by antiaircraft guns. Under

Yamamoto, carriers had developed a system of combat air patrol of fighter planes to attack bombers before they arrived, yet what would happen if the enemy battleships came upon the Japanese carriers when their planes were aloft?

It would never happen, said Yamamoto. The aircraft of the carriers would attack from a point 200 or 300 miles from the position of the battleship. The surface ships would play no role in the battle except as victims. And if by some chance the American fleet should be out, and come within range of the Japanese fleet before the air attack could be made, then the Japanese battleships and cruisers and submarines would destroy the American fleet.

That latter was no more than a hypothetical possibility in Yamamoto's mind. He was the most advanced thinker of the admirals of any nation in the matter of naval air power and its potential, and he had been working on this idea of air power for twenty years. As chief of the navy air army's technological branch at one point, Yamamoto had been instrumental in development of what by 1940 were the most effective torpedo bombers, dive-bombers (better than the German Stuka), and carrier-based fighter planes of any navy.

All of his thoughts had come together on November 13, 1940, when the British had sent slow, ungainly Fairey torpedo planes against the Italian fleet at Taranto, Italy, and had put several major fleet elements out of commission. The strike was a complete success, proving against all comers that airplanes could knock out battleships. And Yamamoto was well aware of the fact that the aircraft at his disposal were far more effective than British torpedo planes.

Yamamoto was a busy man these days. He told the Emperor that the Japanese navy had to be much enlarged, with twice as many carriers and twice as many aircraft. He went back to the fleet and began talking to his chief of staff, Rear Admiral Shigeru Fukudome, and the name Pearl Harbor kept coming up in the conversation. The conventional wisdom of the day to deal with Pearl Harbor had always been to surround it by submarines and then for the Japanese I-boats to attack the American fleet units as they debouched from the confines of the harbor.

Yamamoto thought this was a very shortsighted idea. At the end of 1940 Yamamoto turned over the idea of a Pearl Harbor air attack to Rear Admiral Takejiro Ohnishi. It was not an easy task because at first Ohnishi, like so many others, thought that Yamamoto was out of his mind. But he knew Yamamoto well enough to say so, and Yamamoto knew what he was planning well enough to give a persuasive argument to another skilled airman.

"We may lose five or six carriers in such an attack," said Ohnishi.

"But if we do not make a preemptive strike and knock out the U.S. fleet, we shall be on an equal footing with the Americans to start with," said Yamamoto. And then he went on to discuss

American productive capacity, about which he knew perhaps more than any other person in the Japanese defense establishment, having visited Detroit, other American production centers, and the Mexican and Southwest American oil fields in the 1920s when he served as Japanese naval attaché in Washington.

Besides, Yamamoto told Ohnishi, it was quite right to expect heavy losses. Half a dozen carriers might be lost. But if they sent their aircraft and they had done their job, the sacrifice was worth it. The American fleet would be out of the way, unable to interfere in Japan's planning, and the remainder of the Japanese fleet could carry on from there. One basic trick in Yamamoto's bag had been the buildup of Japanese shore-based naval aviation. If the carriers were gone, Japanese naval airfields in Indochina, China, Taiwan, and the Ryukus could give support for Japanese army operations as far as Malaya and the Philippines.

Yamamoto's arguments convinced Admiral Ohnishi, and from a scoffer he became a convert. He began to consider the Yamamoto plan at the end of 1940 and soon came up with a supportive report saying that the plan was not only possible but that it was extremely desirable. Since Ohnishi had strong contacts in Tokyo with the Naval General Staff, it was not long before the younger element in the general staff was coming around to approval. The admirals were another matter, and this problem would have to be approached through the usual naval channels. Yamamoto's plan for employing aircraft carriers as the major elements of the Japanese fleet demanded a whole new fleet doctrine.

Chapter 3

War Plans

After Admiral Isoroku Yamamoto succeeded Admiral Zengo Yoshida as commander of the Japanese Combined Fleet, his first task was to rebuild the fleet, from a battleship fleet to a carrier-oriented fleet. Since Japan had about the same ratio of battleship admirals to carrier admirals, in terms of thinking, this was not an entirely easy task. Certainly Yamamoto had to pay homage to the past, for the great ships *Yamato* and *Musashi* at 76,000 tons, the largest in the world, were completed and about to be added to the fleet, the *Yamato* to be the new flagship. Admiral Yamamoto, however, saw in the British action at Taranto, when the cream of the Italian fleet was crippled by the planes from a single carrier, that the future of naval war lay with the carrier. He had thought as much for a long time, but here was proof he could use in Tokyo to amplify and press his position. At this time the Japanese Navy had ten aircraft carriers, six fleet carriers, and four light carriers, compared to the American eight carriers, three of which were in the Atlantic, and the Zero carrier fighters and the Nakajima torpedo bombers, the best carrier fighting planes in the Pacific. Only in the American SBD dive-bomber did the U.S. fleet have a weapon that could match the Japanese. The American F4F fighter was a good aircraft, and armored, while the Zero fighter was not, but it did not have the range or the speed to compete with the Zero very successfully.

In the fall of 1940 Yamamoto made his last statement, warning about the negative consequences for Japan of a war against the United States. It came at a chance meeting with Prime Minister Fumimaro Konoye at the Imperial Palace, where both were paying their respects. Konoye asked Yamamoto what he thought about the prospects of the war that was approaching and what would happen at sea if it came.

"I can run wild across the Pacific for six months or a year after war beginnings," he said, "but after that the American productive capacity will begin to show. We will almost certainly lose a war against America."

Konoye was not very pleased with that statement, and others in Japan were not either. Yamamoto realized with the signing of the Tripartite Alliance with Germany and Italy that fall that Japan was committed to war with the United States, and he also realized that it was his responsibility to do the best he could to win it, or to retire from the service. He could certainly have done so; in 1940 Yamamoto had thirty-six years of continual service in the navy. But it was not his way to resign, or to fail in his obligations to the Emperor, which he felt most deeply. Japan's battle plan, as of 1940, was called Kantai Kessen, which meant "decisive battle." All the Japanese planning then (and basically all during the war) called for the Combined Fleet somehow to come to grips with the American fleet and take everything in one great battle. The Japanese were confident that in any such battle, which they preferred to fight at night, they would defeat the Americans. With the defeat of the American fleet, then, the United States would have no way of opposing Japan's efforts in China and the Western Pacific.

The Japanese battle plan was basically offensive, while the American Plan Orange was primarily defensive and based on the realities of the naval situation that had developed since the Japanese began their furious building program in the failure of the London Naval Conference of 1934. The Americans and the British had stood firm for the five-five-three ratio of ships (five American, five British, three Japanese), and the Japanese had refused to accept this second-class position. They considered themselves to be the primary power of the Pacific. When the Allies refused to accept that position, the Japanese broke off the negotiations and began building ships. Five years later they had the more powerful navy in the Pacific without question. Therefore Plan Orange had to be adjusted, and was in March 1941. At that time it was decided in Washington that in the war that was certainly coming, the primary American and British effort must be made to defeat Germany and that American strategy in Asia would be defensive.

The Americans did not want to challenge the Japanese in open battle until such time as they could achieve a better ratio of ships to ships and have a better chance of winning an encounter.

In May 1941, here was the lineup of the American force in the Pacific, as compared to Japan:

	U.S. Pacific Fleet	U.S. Asiatic Fleet	Total	Japan
Battleships	9	0	9	10
Carriers	3	0	3	10
Heavy cruisers	12	1	13	18
Light cruisers	9	2	11	17
Destroyers	67	13	80	111
Submarines	27	28	55	64

Since the Japanese strength outnumbered that of the American forces in the Pacific in every category, it was obvious that the Americans were not going to seek a major naval battle. Therefore the American war plan was based on the loss of the western Pacific and the Philippines, in the first phase of warfare, and a long fight across the Central Pacific to Japan to win the war.

This was a considered policy, established in connection with the British and based on the perception of President Roosevelt that Hitler's Germany was the primary enemy of world peace, and that Hitler had to be dealt with first. Because of that, President Roosevelt resisted military proposals to strengthen American defenses in Alaska and the Pacific. After the *Panay* incident of 1937 on the Yangtze River, he ordered the American gunboats to make themselves scarce on the river, so as not to antagonize the Japanese. All of these were plays for time, for the American eye was on the Atlantic. By 1941, American assistance to Britain in the war against the U-boats had become active, and American ships were employed in escorting British convoys partway across the Atlantic.

In December 1938, the Japanese had announced their intentions to push the white man from Asia with the Greater East Asia Co-Prosperity Sphere. One last chance was given Chiang Kai-shek's China to come into the fold, and when he refused, Japan declared a battle to the death with Chiang, taking steps to set up an alternative Chinese government at the prewar capital of Nanking. It might have been a formidable rival to Chiang Kai-shek — its leader, Wang Ching-wei, had been the close political confidant of Dr. Sun Yat-sen — but the Chinese almost immediately perceived the new Nanking government as a puppet of the Japanese, so arrogant and bald was the Japanese army program in China, and the incipient support began to desert Wang Ching-wei.

While firmly continuing support of Chiang Kai-shek's government in Chongqing, the United States still tried to show Japan that it wished to be conciliatory and settle the outstanding differences. At the end of February 1939 a well-known Japanese member of the diplomatic corps, Admiral Hiroshi Saito, died while in the United States, and the U.S. government decided to send his body back to Japan aboard an American warship as a gesture of respect and amity. Saito had been ambassador to the United States, and very popular for his pro-American views.

The voyage was carried out with all the formalities by Captain Richmond Kelly Turner of the cruiser *Astoria* from March 18 when the ashes of the ambassador were received at Annapolis, accompanied by the Second Secretary of the Japanese Embassy in Washington. The ship stopped at Balboa in the Canal Zone and the Japanese community came to pay respects. The *Astoria* then steamed to Honolulu. After two days, the ship then moved out, bound for Yokohama. As it entered Yokohama harbor on April 17, the *Astoria* bore the American flag at half-mast at the stern and the Japanese flag flying from the fore. The *Astoria* then was escorted by three Japanese destroyers, and in the harbor her twenty-one-gun salute was answered by the Japanese cruiser *Kiso*.

Thousands of Japanese lined the streets to pay

their respects to the ambassador, and a funeral procession moved through downtown Tokyo. The newspapers and newsreels covered the event thoroughly, poets wrote poems about Japanese-American friendship, and singers sang songs praising peace and America. In the next few days thousands of Japanese visited the *Astoria*. A special song was composed about the event.

This day the storms forget to rave.
The angels walk from wave to wave.
This ship glides gently over the foam
That brings the noble envoy home.

Pale blossoms greet you
Seamen from afar
Who bring him home
Where all his memories are.

Welcome you men with hearts so true,
America's best, America's pride.
You show that though the winds blow
That peace and goodwill the storm can ride.

Party followed party, in this joint effort by the Japanese Navy and the American Embassy to show goodwill. War Minister General Itagaki came, and Foreign Minister Hachiro Arita, and Navy Minister Mitsumasu Yonai, the latter being the only firm friend of the United States among the three. The speakers of the two houses of the Diet gave a luncheon and the Emperor gave a tea.

Admiral Yamamoto, then navy vice minister, gave a dinner, and so did Admiral Koga, chief of the naval general staff. But far more impressive than the official reaction, which was formal and proper, was the reaction of the Japanese people, who cheered and blessed the Americans, and many of whom cried as they stood watching the parades. One old lady walked up to a junior officer and kissed him on the cheek.

The goodwill of the Japanese people was real, as could be seen. The government's position was typical of the time under army control. The army said privately that the whole affair was a slap in the face by President Roosevelt to the Japanese government, because Admiral Saito had been in disfavor with the army oligarchy, who had secured his dismissal from his ambassadorial post. His crime: He had apologized prematurely to the Americans for the sinking of the gunboat *Panay* on the Yangtze River. So, in effect, the whole affair was what the Japanese call *shibai*, a drama performed for effect, one that had absolutely no bearing on the policies of military Japan, which were already inexorably set on the Pan Asia course.

By the spring of 1939 the Imperial Japanese Army was well on its way in planning the opening moves of the Pacific war. Shortly before the *Astoria* had sailed on her goodwill mission, the Japanese had occupied Hainan Island, which would be the base from which the invasion of Malaya would be launched. All of mainland China's major cities in the east had been occupied by the Japanese by then, and they were preparing to shut down Chiang's lifelines to the west, the roads and railroads from northern Indochina and the Burma road over the Himalayas to Kunming.

American public opinion swung squarely behind China much faster than the American government, but the old Treaty of Commerce with Japan was denounced, and in 1940 the American government began issuing a series of moves against Japanese trade that hurt. Admiral Turner, then advanced into the naval staff planning section, warned that economic sanctions would make the Japanese decide on a course of war, but Admiral Harold Stark, the chief of naval operations, advocated them.

By this time the two governments were moving on a collision course: The Japanese insisted that they must have a free hand to bring China "to her senses" and make her the focal point of the Greater East Asia Co-Prosperity Sphere. The Americans insisted that the Japanese withdraw entirely from China. Since trade had followed the flag and Japanese investment had followed conquest, it was totally unrealistic of the Americans to insist on this blanket withdrawal, and the Japanese saw that attitude as the beginning action in the war. By the spring of 1941 the American Pacific Fleet had moved to Pearl Harbor, which the Japanese saw as an open threat against them, and the Americans and British and Australians were conferring on joint action in the Pacific. On April

21 they began a series of meetings at Singapore with the Dutch, which the Japanese saw as "encirclement."

The Americans denied time and again that they had any definite plans for defense of the Dutch-Malay area, but the Japanese knew the denials were false and they only increased the Japanese suspicion and moved Japan more firmly toward war.

All of these actions against Japan were overwhelmingly supported by the American people, according to public opinion polls. What the Japanese military seemed unable to grasp was the deep-seated resentment of the American people against Japan's military arrogance, which was a product of the rebuilding of the Japanese Army into an inhuman fighting force. There were too many stories of rape, murder, and looting by Japanese soldiers. No one doubted that these actions were military policy in occupied areas.

Meanwhile in 1940 and 1941 affairs moved steadily toward war. In July the British closed down the Burma road under pressure from Japan and in September 1940, the Japanese moved into French Indochina. The United States suspended all oil shipments to Japan, which deprived her of her supply source. From now until she got another source she would be eating into her slender oil reserves. On September 27 the Japanese signed the Tripartite Pact, which was an open alliance with Germany and Italy against the United States. The major elements of the navy were still working for an agreement between the United States and Japan, and the appointment of Admiral Kichisaburo Nomura as ambassador to the United States was as far as the navy could press in that direction against the Gunbatsu, the military junta.

Admiral Nomura's task was virtually impossible, given the mind-set of the Japanese government and that of the American government, but he tried nobly. Besides his official diplomacy, he met with as many Americans in high places as he could and explained to them his conviction that the best interest of both countries would be served by maintaining the peace. One day in March, he talked with Admiral Turner at a party at the Japanese Embassy and said he would like to talk further. Next day he called Turner and arranged for a meeting that day.

At the meeting, Nomura was frank. The war in China and the other bellicose behavior of the Japanese government, he said, was the responsibility of the young radical officers in the Japanese Army. The senior officers, on the contrary, had been and still were in favor of peace with the United States. This was true but it did not help much because the younger officers, many of them only majors and lieutenant colonels, seemed to manipulate their seniors with ease.

Admiral Turner left the meeting with the feeling that Admiral Nomura would do his best to prevent Japan from making more aggressive military moves, which indeed he did do. His last important act was to transmit a personal message to Emperor Hirohito. Had that message been delivered, the war probably would not have occurred when it did, for it was most conciliatory. But the "young officers" who were in charge of Imperial General Headquarters made sure the message was not delivered until after war was actually declared.

So one could say that Admiral Nomura was on the side of the angels, although his efforts came to naught. He and Admiral Turner held several meetings. Nomura said frankly that the Japanese economic situation had been badly hurt by the American economic sanctions, and that Japan felt she would have to take action soon to rectify the problems created.

Admiral Turner digested that information and warned his superiors that if they wanted to avoid war, or so long as they wanted to avoid war, they should go slow on any more economic blows against Japan; that country's slender economy would not stand them, and the decision for war might be forthcoming at any time.

On April 13, 1941, the Japanese signed the Russo-Japanese nonaggression pact, which gave the Japanese a license to move south against Malaya and the Dutch East Indies. By July 1941, Japan had occupied all of French Indochina, and that month the United States closed ports to Japanese trade. For months the Japanese and Americans had been "negotiating" to try to solve their differences, but it was apparent that the differences were insoluble by negotiation. From the American point of view, they would have to give up their support of China and let Japan have control of East Asia. From the Japanese point of view, the Western powers would have to agree to get out of Asia and leave it to the Asians.

In the summer, the Japanese wanted Prince Konoye to come to Washington. The Americans refused to see him, a decision made in the Department of State. There was talk about a personal meeting with President Roosevelt, and he favored it, but the professionals in the diplomatic and military service managed to get the idea quashed.

What might have happened had Konoye and Roosevelt met will never be known, but it is known that Konoye, with all his faults, was a man of international understanding and goodwill, and F.D.R. had a strong feeling for the rights of man and a sympathy for the will of colonial peoples to be free. The Pan Asianism of Japan might not have disturbed him as much as it did the professional diplomats and military men who spent the next quarter of a century still thinking in terms of protecting the status quo and existing power blocs. But nothing happened, and the sop that came, the dispatch of another Japanese diplomat to assist Admiral Kurusu, helped nothing at all.

On September 6, 1941, the Japanese made their decision for war with the United States at a liaison conference held between representatives of the government, then headed by Prince Konoye, and the military, who seemingly held equal power with the government but actually bad control, because no government could survive without a war minister, and the army had the power to withdraw the war minister any time it disagreed with government policy.

The Konoye cabinet persisted until October 16, when it collapsed and was succeeded by a cabinet led by General Hideki Tojo. Specifically Tojo had been enjoined by Emperor Hirohito to start anew in considering problems vis-à-vis the United States, but in fact the decision made on September 6 would be reaffirmed in October.

Here is the justification by the Japanese government and army for their decision for war, as written down by the secretaries of the liaison conference, as *aides memoires* for the prime minister to answer questions that might be propounded in behalf of the Emperor:

Question: Is war with Great Britain and the United States inevitable?

Answer: Our Empire's plan to build a New Order in East Asia — the central problem of which is the settlement of the China Incident — is a firm policy based on the national principle of *Hakko ichiu* (eight corners of the world under one roof). The building of the New Order will go on forever, much as the life of our State does.

However, it appears that the policy of the United States toward Japan is based on the idea of preserving the status quo; in order to dominate the world and defend democracy, it aims to prevent our Empire from rising and developing in East Asia. Under these circumstances, it must be pointed out that the policies of Japan and the United States are mutually incompatible; it is historically inevitable, that the conflict between the two countries, which is sometimes intense and sometimes moderate, will ultimately lead to war.

It need not be repeated that unless the United States changes its policy toward Japan, our Empire is placed in a desperate situation, where it must resort to the ultimate step — namely, war — to defend itself and assure its preservation. Even if we should make concessions to the United States by giving up part of our national policy for the sake of temporary peace, the United States, its military position strengthened, is sure to demand more and more concessions on our part, and ultimately our Empire will have to lie prostrate at the feet of the United States.

And so on September 6, 1941, the clock began to tick, and although there were a few hesitations between that day and December 7, 1941, the clock never stopped.

Chapter 4

The Japanese Plan

In December 1940, Admiral Yamamoto had decided that affairs in Japan had progressed to the point that war with the Western nations was inevitable. Having accepted that fact, it was not hard for him to turn all his efforts to find some way in which the Japanese Navy had at least a chance of assuring the national salvation. Yamamoto still stood on the "run amok" statement he had made to Prime Minister Konoye, but he was a realist, not a fatalist, and if there was a way for Japan to win a victory he was going to try to find it. On January 7, 1941, Yamamoto wrote a letter to Navy Minister Admiral Kashiro Oikawa, outlining his general plan . . . preemptive strike at Pearl Harbor . . . employing the First and Second Carrier divisions if possible . . . blockade the harbor . . . decide the fate of the war on the first day . . . tankers for refueling at sea . . . destroyers to rescue survivors of ships sunk by counterattack. . . . He also noted that it was possible that the American fleet would come out and meet them before they got to Pearl Harbor. So much the better, and furthermore, he, Yamamoto, wanted to take personal command of the air fleet that made the attack.

A few days after Yamamoto had sent his letter to Admiral Oikawa, he wrote a personal letter to Admiral Takejiro Ohnishi, chief of staff of the Eleventh Air Fleet at Kanoya air base in Kyushu, and a personal friend and one of the most innovative men in the Japanese Navy. Ohnishi came to see Yamamoto aboard the flag-ship *Nagato* in Ariake Bay in southern Kyushu about two weeks later. They talked about the technical difficulties (such matters as getting torpedoes to run true in the shallow water of the harbor), and then Admiral Ohnishi went back to his headquarters to work up the details. His senior staff officer said it couldn't be done, and he cited the difficulty about the torpedoes.

Admiral Ohnishi was not dismayed. He knew the man who would welcome the idea and be capable of doing the spadework in the planning. He was Commander Minoru Genda, then air officer on the carrier *Kaga*. Genda came to Kanoya, listened, and was convinced that the scheme was possible, although difficult. He also had some amplifications: several strikes should be made to do the job properly. It would start with two waves of attackers, from six carriers, an entirely new idea in naval air warfare.

Late in February 1941, Commander Genda returned to Kanoya with the elements of a plan: a surprise attack, with the carriers the main objective and also the land-based aircraft on Oahu Island, to secure air superiority over the target from the outset. They must have as many carriers as possible, six at least. All types of attack should be made: level bombing, dive-bombing, and torpedo bombing.

As the Naval General Staff pondered the Pearl Harbor attack plan, which was an adaptation of Admiral Heihachiro Togo's preemptive strike on the Russian Fleet at Port Arthur in 1904, Yamamoto kept the Combined Fleet at sea most of the time, doubling and redoubling the training program. He wanted his ship captains to be so used to night operations that there would never be an error, so night after night, his blacked-out ships went into and out of port. Back in Tokyo Admiral Ohnishi fought the battle of the admirals, his principal target being Admiral Kashiro Oikawa, the navy minister. The reason was that if the Yamamoto plan was to be followed there would have to be major changes in the organization of the fleet, building it around a carrier striking force, instead of a battleship striking force. Obviously there was some strong opposition, particularly since the two 76,000-ton battleships *Yamato* and *Musashi* were nearly ready for the fleet, and three more were planned, one of them half completed. (That was the *Shinano*, whose design was changed to make her an aircraft carrier, the largest in the world.)

By April 1941, Admiral Yamamoto had several projects in the works at navy headquarters. One was the Pearl Harbor attack, but to carry it out, there must first be a reorganization of the Combined Fleet. On April 10, this came about when the navy organized the First Air Fleet, with five carriers. The rub was that the man chosen by seniority to command this new First Air Fleet did not know anything about carriers. He was Vice Admiral Chuichi Nagumo. Like so many battleship admirals he was half afraid of carriers and desperately afraid of losing them in battle.

In April and May the airmen who would make the attack on Pearl Harbor trained hard. Early in June, Commander Genda launched an intensive torpedo training program at Kagoshima, on Kyushu Island, where the layout was quite similar to that at Pearl Harbor. There the fliers practiced techniques of dropping torpedoes for short runs in shallow water, not quite knowing why they were doing so. Meanwhile the torpedo experts were modifying the Japanese naval aerial torpedo to make it run better in shallow water.

The level bombing training was also very technical and very complete, even to the presentation of a special steel target that was the same quality as the armor of the American battleships. Practicing horizontal bombing on the old battleship *Settsu*, the twin-engined bombers averaged three to five hits with 1,500-pound bombs for every nine bombs dropped from 12,000 feet.

As of August, although the Combined Fleet

was training every day for the Pearl Harbor operation, it had not yet been accepted by the Naval General Staff, which still clung to the old battleship planning. Yamamoto sent an emissary to Tokyo to try to persuade the admirals and their bright young men of the staff. There were still many unanswered questions, among them the problem of sending a fleet so far from home to fight and then bringing it back home again. But Yamamoto had answers: refuel at sea was the answer to that one, and although it had not been done before by the Japanese Navy, all the techniques were known. There was nothing impossible about it, even in changeable weather. It took some planning, that was all.

Although the operation was still top secret, word about it had seeped down through the Japanese military establishment, and in fact, American Ambassador Joseph Grew had been told by another diplomat that such a plan was in the works, although he could get no confirmation or detail about it. In navy circles they began to call it Operation Hawaii. Although the Naval General Staff still had not given the go-ahead, the plan was gathering its own steam. Admiral Yamamoto had no doubt that in the end he would get the approval, so sure was he that this was the only sensible way to approach the Americans.

Early in September, Admiral Nagumo's First Air Fleet staff was informed of the Yamamoto plans and Commander Genda was named head of the group of officers assigned to study all the questions about the operation and come up with all the answers.

That month in the shifting of personnel within the navy, Yamamoto lost his chief of staff, Admiral Ito, who became deputy to Admiral Nagano, chief of the Naval General Staff. So now two of Yamamoto's old chiefs of staff were in high places in the Imperial Naval Staff.

Still, Yamamoto did not have approval of the Pearl Harbor plan, but he had indications that it would be forthcoming. The Naval General Staff in September ordered a model of Oahu Island be constructed, and the war games, usually slated for October, were moved up this year because Yamamoto wanted to show the value of his Pearl Harbor plan.

On September 11, 1941, Admiral Yamamoto and the staff of the Combined Fleet traveled up to Tokyo to the Imperial Naval Staff College, took over a room in the east wing of the building, and rehearsed the attack on Pearl Harbor in what they called "tabletop" exercises. From September 12 to September 16, the exercises went on every day, beginning at 8:00 A.M. and ending at 5 P.M. One team carried out the attack plan of the Japanese and another represented the enemy. The war games covered the whole gamut of the Japanese plan of attack, on Malaya, the Philippines, the Dutch East Indies, and, not least of all, Hawaii. That rehearsal was saved for last, in the special room set aside for it on September 16.

Admiral Nagumo was there, worrying with members of his staff. About thirty officers in all attended, from various important naval commands. The Naval General Staff was represented but not by Admiral Nagano.

There were several quarrels. Admiral Nagumo insisted on the easier southern route, although his staff wanted the northern route. Another disagreement developed over aerial reconnaissance on the way to Hawaii. The war games ended with many matters still undecided, the number of carriers, and the question of reconnaissance. Ultimately reconnaissance was abandoned as too dangerous. The gamesters met the next day for a postmortem on their operations, and discussed more fine points. Then they held a dinner, which officially ended the games for Operation Hawaii. Admiral Nagano had still not said that they could go, but everyone was counting on it, except Admiral Nagumo, who had not liked the idea from the beginning and now was beginning to find out that it was real, not just a Yamamoto pipe dream. He was not visibly encouraged when Admiral Fukudome said to him cheerily, "If you die in this operation special shrines will be built in your memory."

Admiral Fukudome, from the start, had believed that the whole Pearl Harbor Operation was extremely risky and might endanger the whole fleet. Yamamoto admitted all this, but, he said, if you want to beat the Americans you have got to take the risk. Otherwise it is just a question of time until the Americans would come and get the Japanese fleet.

Admiral Nagano at this point made his first observation on the whole plan. "In case of war I do not favor launching operations as risky as Yamamoto's plan. I think it is best for the navy to limit its plans and concentrate on capturing the southern regions."

The Operations Section of Naval General Headquarters shared that view; they did not want anything to do with Yamamoto's plan.

Underlying all this was one major change in attitude. After the war games, everyone in the naval high command seemed to realize that the economic situation of Japan was growing desperate, pushed by the American sanctions, and that if they did not go to war within the next six months, they might as well surrender to the Americans without fighting because they would have no oil with which to fight.

Now came one of those events that guides Japanese destiny. On September 24, Admiral Fukudome, now of the Naval General Staff, and Admiral Ugaki, now Yamamoto's chief of staff, called a meeting at the operations section of the General Staff. It was not attended by any commanders, just staff members, for they wanted to speak openly and without the usual toadying to their superiors.

This routine was actually how the Japanese Navy worked. The staff officers sorted out the details, leaving only the major decisions to the top admirals. So both sides were represented very well. Ugaki believed he had to "out Yamamoto" his commander, and it was the same with others — their loyalties were firm. The conference took almost all day. Fukudome, the General Staff man, presided, and although he did not like the plan he said nothing. But Admiral Kusaka, Nagumo's chief of staff, said that the plan was no good. And the others of the Nagumo staff brought up one objection after another — fueling problems and fears that bombing could not sink all those ships and that the Americans would have them repaired in a trice. But Genda, the airman, did not share these fears. He hoped to sink eight battleships, he said. They had the level bombers, which performed beautifully, and torpedo bombers, which were still having their troubles, as were the dive-bombers. But Genda was going for the torpedo bombing. This was, he said, the way to deal with the American fleet.

They talked about the date, if the Pearl Harbor operation was going to come off at all, and this posed a problem. Yamamoto wanted the strike on a Sunday morning, when most of the American ships should be at anchor. He was thinking of striking on November 20, but the Naval General Staff said this was too early, and Admiral Kusaka, speaking for Nagumo, agreed.

That last word was that of Admiral Fukudome, representing the General Staff. He said that the meeting had been very instructive and that soon the General Staff would make the decision: Hawaii or no Hawaii. When Yamamoto heard this opinion he erupted. Did not those fools in Tokyo know that the U.S. fleet must be crippled if all else was to succeed?

But now Yamamoto faced some new problems. For one thing Admiral Ohnishi began to be less enthusiastic about the Pearl Harbor attack plan. One reason was that Ohnishi faced the prospect of having to carry out attacks on the Philippines with a sharply reduced force, because so many aircraft would be required for the Pearl Harbor project. Also, he had been talking to Admiral Kusaka, the chief of staff to Admiral Nagumo, and they were both very much opposed to the whole scheme as too risky. (For the men who would undertake the mission to have such a feeling was not very comforting to Yamamoto nor did it augur well for the success of the raid.)

At the end of September Kusaka and Ohnishi called on Yamamoto and made their objections to the plan. Yamamoto did not lose his temper. Instead he told them that he was determined on the plan, that his whole Pacific war plan depended on it, and that he needed their help. It was just the sort of appeal that changed men's minds, and both Ohnishi and Kusaka left Yamamoto that day vowing to do their utmost to further the plan that neither of them wanted to undertake.

On October 2, aboard the *Kaga*, which was serving as his temporary flagship, Admiral Nagumo announced the Hawaii mission to the senior members of his First Air Fleet. By

October 10, the ships and the men and the pilots of the planes that would make the attack were assembling. In Tokyo the army and the navy high commands had both come to the same conclusion that there was no further gain to be made in the continuing negotiations with America. War was the only answer, and both army and navy men had a sense of urgency about the necessity for action.

On October 12, a Sunday, Prime Minister Konoye met with the four key members of his cabinet, War Minister Tojo, Foreign Minister Toyoda, Navy Minister Oikawa, and the president of the Planning Board, Suzuki. When the army and navy ministers made it clear they were insisting on war, and that if Prime Minister Konoye would not lead them into war, then they must have a leader who would. At that point Konoye decided to resign, and by October 16 he had resigned, much to the surprise and displeasure of the Emperor, who was now faced with war clouds he did not want.

On that same day Admiral Yamamoto held a special rehearsal of Operation Hawaii aboard the Combined Fleet flagship *Nagato*. The tabletop maneuvers of the previous month in Tokyo were repeated, and that evening all those concerned stayed aboard the flagship for dinner. On October 13, the top admirals involved and their staffs met with Yamamoto. Several of these admirals spoke up against launching the attack.

Then Yamamoto stood up. He had been

studying the attack plan for a long time, he said. He had listened to all that had been said on this day and on other occasions and he realized that many officers did not agree with his plan. But, he added, the Hawaii operation was a very definite part of Japan's grand naval strategy and so long as he was commander-in-chief of the fleet it would go ahead.

"I ask you to give me your fullest support. Return to your stations and work hard for the success of Japan's war plan. Good luck."

On the tactical level there was nothing more to say. If the attack was to be called off now it would have to be by the naval high command in Tokyo, who, after all this time and all this argument, refused to accept Yamamoto's strategic concept.

At this point, the high command was still dragging its feet. Now there was talk about making the raid with only three carriers, an idea that Yamamoto opposed vigorously, but Nagumo, who did not want to go at all, favored it because it meant less risk and less responsibility. Admiral Yamamoto's planners were now figuring on an attack on December 8 (December 7, Hawaii time), but still nothing was settled. But in the last few weeks, Yamamoto had brought Admiral Kusaka, Nagumo's chief of staff, around to supporting the mission and Kusaka now was convinced that six carriers were needed to provide a massive air raid.

In Tokyo, naval headquarters opposed the six-carrier strike because they said at least two carriers were needed for the southern operations that would be carried out simultaneously. Kusaka returned from Tokyo to see Yamamoto a very dispirited man. But Yamamoto told him not to despair, he would now force the issue. On October 18, he sent Captain Kemeto Kurishima to Tokyo, armed with all Yamamoto's facts and figures, and a secret weapon. Kurishima trotted out the facts and figures, but Rear Admiral Sadashi Tomioka, the chief of operations of the Naval General Staff, had heard all these arguments and was not convinced by them. He still opposed the Hawaii operation.

And Captain Kurishima said what Yamamoto had instructed him to say if matters came to impasse: "Admiral Yamamoto insists that his plan be adopted. I am authorized to state that if it is not, then the Commander in Chief of the Combined Fleet can no longer be held responsible for the security of the Empire. In that case he will have no alternative but to resign and with him his entire staff."

That was a shocker!

For if there was a national hero in Japan, it was Admiral Yamamoto, beloved of the people and of the navy.

That statement changed things around. Admiral Tomioka's opposition simply evaporated (and with it the opposition of the entire general staff, because as operations officer in this he was the key figure). He did, however, make three conditions: that only six carriers would be used in the operation and that no more be requested, that no more aircraft be demanded from the supply line before the operation, and that as soon as possible after the Hawaii Operation the First Air Fleet would be available for operations in the south.

Captain Kurishima could have virtually assured Admiral Tomioka of Yamamoto's concurrence in all three provisos, but Tomioka wanted it in writing so he got it that way. Then Kurishima went in, to beard Admiral Fukudome, who was Tomioka's chief. Once again he had to take recourse in Yamamoto's threat to quit to get by that hurdle. After Fukudome, Tomioka and Kurishima went to see Admiral Ito, now deputy chief of the Naval General Staff. He heard, and without further ado took Tomioka into Admiral Nagano to confer while Kurishima waited in Ito's office.

Admiral Nagano had never liked the Pearl Harbor plan, and he did not like it now, but rather than have Yamamoto resign, he agreed to let the impetuous admiral have his head.

And so the issue was decided, almost at the eleventh hour. Nagano, too, made conditions: that the Pearl Harbor attack not adversely affect the southern operation in any way, timing or other, and second, that nothing be done to take the air strength of the navy for any subsidiary purpose, to weaken the southern air attack.

Thus Admiral Yamamoto had won, it appeared, but there could still be slips. So it was not until early November, when the Yamamoto Pearl Harbor plan was incorporated into Combined

Fleet Operation Order No. 1 from Naval General Headquarters, that Yamamoto could breathe that final sigh of relief and get on with the war.

Meanwhile the detailed planning went ahead. The fleet flagship *Nagato* sailed to Saeki Bay on October 20, and Admiral Yamamoto and his staff began conferring with the admirals who would lead the First Air Fleet, the submarines, and the auxiliary ships that would come along in support. Next day the Naval General Staff issued the first war directive. The date December 8 was set for operations.

Now the big problem was Admiral Nagumo, whom Yamamoto knew to still oppose the Hawaii Operation. Chief of Staff Ugaki suggested to Yamamoto that if Nagumo did not think he could carry out the orders happily, he should resign. Yamamoto agreed, but there was no way Yamamoto could force the issue because the Nagumo appointment had been made through the naval hierarchy. Yamamoto had never even been consulted on it, as he did not expect to be, given the Japanese naval system. Admiral Yamamoto had talked earlier of getting rid of any admiral who did not wholeheartedly support the operations, but to do so would be to create a new and perhaps lasting crisis within the navy. Even Yamamoto backed away from that.

To put the cap on the success, Admiral Yamamoto wrote a letter to the new navy minister in the new Tojo cabinet that had succeeded Prince Konoye's. Yamamoto knew Tojo from of old, when they had been navy and army deputy ministers years ago, and he knew that Tojo was one of the most loyal of the Gunbatsu's servants. So he also knew that Tojo would opt for war. Still he could not help but write Shimada one last time protesting the coming war against the West.

He said he had still been hearing from Tokyo that people on the Naval General Staff were concerned about using so much of the naval air force for what was actually a secondary operation, not directly connected with the joint army-navy move south, particularly since, as Yamamoto put it, the chances were not more than fifty-fifty that the Pearl Harbor operation would succeed. That, he said, because he had a great respect for Admiral Husband E. Kimmel, the commander of the U.S. Pacific Fleet, and he was not at all sure what war plan Kimmel would follow, or even how he would react to the attack on Pearl Harbor. "It does not appear to me likely that the American Navy will necessarily confine itself to the strategy of a steady frontal offensive," he said.

"But even more risky and illogical, it seems to me, is the idea of going to war against America, Britain and China, following four years of exhausting operations in China, with the possibility of fighting Russia also to be kept in mind, and having, moreover, to sustain ourselves unassisted for ten years or more in a protracted war over an area several times more vast than the European war theater. In the face of such odds, if we decide to go to war — or rather are forced to do so by the trend of events — I, as the authority responsible for the fleet, can see little hope of success in any ordinary strategy."

So it was to be all or nothing, and the blow at Pearl Harbor was intended to sink the American carriers, first of all, then the battleships and auxiliary ships, and to leave Pearl Harbor in such a condition that the American Navy could not interfere with Japanese operations in the South Pacific for many, many months.

Chapter 5

How Ready Can Ready Be?

In January 1941, very shortly after Admiral Yamamoto had first proposed a preemptive strike on Pearl Harbor, the first secretary of the U.S. Embassy in Tokyo was tipped off by a friend in the diplomatic corps that such a plan was afoot and went straight to Ambassador Joseph Grew with the message. On January 27, Ambassador Grew sent a coded warning to Washington. But in Washington the message was regarded as a laughing matter. "However could Grew be taken in by such nonsense?" was the question.

But somebody in the Navy Department decided at least to cover himself, and so the message was sent to the commander in chief of the U.S. Pacific Fleet, by way of Commander Arthur McCollum, of the Far East Section of Naval Intelligence Operations. McCollum was not surprised. He was an old Far East hand, born in Japan of missionary parents. Besides, the American war plan and war games had for years rested on the assumption that one of the first acts of the Japanese in war would be to strike Pearl Harbor to destroy the naval facilities there. The idea was so old it was laughable, and therefore it was not believable. Commander McCollum did not believe it, and he sent the message to Admiral Husband E. Kimmel, commander in chief of the U.S. Pacific Fleet, with this aside: "The Division of Naval Intelligence places no credence in the rumors. . . ."

And neither did the army, which had precisely the same mind-set. So many magazine articles had been written over the years with the scenario of a Japanese attack on Pearl Harbor that responsible navy and army officers just could not bring themselves to consider that it might be a reality.

But where Commander McCollum's message led Admiral Kimmel astray was at the end:

"Furthermore, based on known data regarding the present disposition and employment of Japanese naval and army forces, no move against Pearl Harbor appears imminent or planned for in the foreseeable future."

If there was ever a message meant to lull, that was it.

Another aspect of the general American attitude, also shared in the military, was contempt for the Japanese. Anti-Oriental feeling ran high in America in the last of the nineteenth century and the first third of the twentieth century. Many Americans did not recognize Orientals as real "people." The American image of the Japanese was a cartoon character — short, bowlegged (some were from rickets), nearsighted, unable to speak English properly (which indicated a lack of brain), inscrutable, always smiling, and very, very crafty. But not inventive. Navy buffs liked to tell the story of the Japanese destroyer that was launched in the 1930s. Beautiful and sleek and an exact copy of the current American destroyers. But because the canny Americans had fooled the Japanese spies who stole the plans, the destroyer was launched and went straight to the bottom of the sea.

The story was not true, of course, but it was told up and down the West Coast and generally believed, because Americans believed the Japanese were masters at espionage and great copiers, although they could not produce anything worthwhile on their own.

This mind-set more than anything else seems to have contributed to the failures that led, one after another, to Pearl Harbor.

But this alone could not have produced a disaster. Other factors had to be working.

One factor was based on more than a little truth. Japan, said the experts, was nearly bankrupt after the recession of 1922, which for the Japanese extended into the 1930s. The failure of crops hurt more, and the Japanese economy was in even worse shape than the Western. All true, but meaningless because in the 1930s Japan was coming under the control of the army, and the money was being found to build weapons and increase the armed forces.

One of the other factors was a general American feeling of well-being and sense of being protected by two broad oceans.

Another was the natural antipathy of Americans to the maintenance of a large standing army and navy. The American military tradition, until the last half of the twentieth century, was always thus. American wars were fought by citizen soldiers, and the feeling persisted in the 1920s and 1930s that this was just fine. Thus Congress whittled away at the defense budget, and then when the depression of the 1930s hit like a hurricane, there simply was no money for military programs.

But when the war in Europe threatened the British lifeline to the Americans, and when Japanese expansion in Asia became more serious than some believed it would with the invasion of Indochina in the fall of 1914, then the American fleet was split and half of it was sent to the West Coast as a deterrent against Japan. In 1940, that half was moved to Pearl Harbor, over the objections of the fleet commander, Admiral J. O. Richardson, a talented but abrasive officer, who had the temerity (and bad judgment) to tell President Roosevelt that the military did not trust the civilians to run foreign and military policy. That was the end of Richardson's command of the fleet. He lasted until January 5, 1941, when he was replaced by Admiral Husband E. Kimmel.

At that time Admiral Kimmel was a rear admiral, serving as commander of cruisers of the fleet battle force.

The successful British attack on the Italian fleet at Taranto had not gone unnoticed by the American navy, and at about this time the navy sent "through channels" a warning to the commander of the Pacific Fleet to beware of the possibility of a Japanese torpedo or bombing attack on the fleet at Pearl Harbor. But that sort of warning, which sounds very good when read in later years, did not mean very much at the time because it was totally impersonal and took a student of history to decipher it the way it was composed.

The reality was the American perception, in February 1941, that "no move against Pearl Harbor appears imminent or planned for the foreseeable future."

When Admiral Kimmel took over, he looked around and immediately wrote Washington, complaining about the minimal protection facilities for the Pacific Fleet at Hawaii. When that complaint reached General George C. Marshall, who was responsible for air defense, he admitted that it was true, but "What Kimmel does not realize is that we are tragically lacking in this materiel throughout the army and that Hawaii is on a far better basis than any other command in the army." Marshall mentioned one other factor that seemed to dominate the military mind those days: sabotage. Because of the activities of a Fifth Column (largely in France and much overrated) in the European war, the American Army high command had a fixation about sabotage that led them to expend far more energy on sabotage protection than on protection from an outside enemy. Sabotage, said General Marshall, was the major threat to the islands.

And from where would that sabotage come? Why from the Japanese and Japanese-Americans living in Hawaii, of course. The army saw in the Japanese a large Fifth Column. The assumption was that all the 160,000 people in Hawaii of Japanese blood were basically Japanese at heart and would not hesitate to attack or help the Japanese any way they could. It was an assumption with no basis in fact whatever, a hangover from the anti-Orientalism that had pervaded America in the late nineteenth century and was still very strong.

The Japanese government used a diplomatic code called Purple in which they had great faith and continued to use all during the prewar period. The Americans had broken the Purple code in 1940 and from that point on read all their messages. This meant specifically that the State Department knew precisely what the Japanese foreign office was saying to the Japanese ambassador in Washington. The U.S. Navy had not yet broken the Japanese naval codes and the Japanese Army codes were still intact, so there was much that the Americans did not know. And at this time and in the future months, one of the greatest difficulties the people in Hawaii would have was the jealousy of the Naval Intelligence Office in Washington, which held that it alone should be the interpreter and carrier of news about Japan's intentions. For was it not *headquarters?* The argument between ONI in Washington and Fleet Intelligence continued until the last, and may even have prejudiced the information processes, as it certainly threatened to do later at the time of the Battle of Midway, when ONI Washington tried to steer Admiral Chester W. Nimitz away from sending ships to fight because, ONI said, the Japanese were going to attack somewhere else.

In the spring of 1941, Admiral Kimmel asked the commander of naval air forces in the Hawaii area, Rear Admiral Patrick Bellinger, commander of Patrol Wing 2, to work out a defense stance for the islands with Major General Frederick Martin of the U.S. Army Air Force. They did work on a report, called the Martin-Bellinger Report, which presupposed a submarine and air attack on Hawaii, and said that the air defenses were not adequate to maintain a patrol extensive enough to prevent the Japanese from coming in and attacking Pearl Harbor. What was needed were enough long-range aircraft to maintain a continual 360-degree patrol around the islands, far enough out at sea so that the patrols would find enemy carriers well before they could launch their planes, and the fleet would be alerted in plenty of time to act.

The document was dated March 31, 1941, which was about the same time that Admiral Yamamoto put his staff to work on the plan for the attack on Pearl Harbor.

Since the study showed that the army and navy together did not have the resources to do the job right, instead of rushing aircraft into production to solve the problem — which there was no way of doing under the American defense system of 1941 — the navy undertook to do the scouting and the army gave up, retaining scouting only 20 miles offshore, which would not have any effect on anything except possibly a submarine attack.

The navy was almost as bad off. The only search planes available were those of Patrol Wing 2, which were not enough to maintain a constant vigil, handicapped as they were by a shortage of pilots and crews.

In that spring of 1941, Admiral Nomura came to Washington as ambassador, hoping to secure a long-term peace through negotiations. He had excellent credentials as a friend of the United States, but he also had to contend with the strong distrust of his country's intentions at every level of the American government, and an equally strong distrust of America that existed in Tokyo to the extent that Nomura was not made party to much that was going on at home. The fact was that through its ability to read Japanese diplomatic messages to places other than Washington, the State Department had a very good idea that Japan's foreign policy was dictated by the army. Even the disappearance from the Japanese cabinet of Foreign Minister Yosuke Matsuoka, the most notorious of America haters, did not mean much change, the Americans decided.

After the Japanese move into southern Indochina at the end of July 1941, President Roosevelt froze Japanese assets in America. An embargo was also put on shipments of oil to Japan. This last was a real shock to the Japanese and an indication to them that the negotiations in Washington were not going to get anywhere. For years the militarists said that this was just what the Americans would do in time of trouble.

Now Japan had the choice of backing down on its declaration that it would fight the China war to a finish with Chiang Kai-shek or sticking to its decision and finding the oil it needed elsewhere.

There was only one readily available source of oil to the Japanese, and that was in the Dutch East Indies. The Indies, belonging to a Holland that had been overrun by the Germans, were trying to continue to function through the Batavia government. But they were already under strong pressure from the Japanese to supply most Japanese oil needs. If the Dutch acquiesced, the Japanese would continue to make greater and greater demands. If they refused, the Japanese would come and take the oil by force. In Washington Admiral Nomura began to worry about the future.

He worried more on July 30 when one of a formation of Japanese naval planes flying over Chungking, China, suddenly broke out of formation and bombed the American gunboat *Tutuila*. There was no question about the intent. The *Tutuila* was showing a big American flag. The bomb narrowly missed. The Americans made a protest through Admiral Nomura. He could tell at the meeting by the set of the American faces that they were very angry.

The Imperial Navy denied responsibility and claimed that this was an unauthorized attack. Of course it was true, but by the summer of 1941 young Japanese officers were doing things like that and getting away with them. In this case the navy apologized promptly and the Americans accepted the apology, but everyone knew that no one meant either. The Japanese might do it again, and as soon as the Americans were ready to act they would act. Affairs in China had reached a point very close to breach of diplomatic relations.

The Americans were playing for time while they built up their defenses. President Roosevelt was also preoccupied with the ever greater American participation in Britain's war against the German U-boats, for the German submarines were threatening Britain's ability to carry on the war. So the Americans took no further action — except to recall General Douglas MacArthur. He was in the Philippines, commander of the Philippine army. He was recalled to duty with the American army and would be in charge of USAFFE — United States Armed Forces, Far East. It was a new command established to warn the Japanese. The Japanese, for their part, took stock of the oil situation, and some heretofore vacillating minds were made up inside the Imperial Navy. For everyone knew that with the oil situation as it was, if Japan delayed until 1942 to make the Pearl Harbor raid, they might not have enough fuel to make it. The whole timetable of the Japanese war schedule was formed that summer, as Japan's military leaders assessed their situation. Either they would get what they wanted (all the American oil they wanted and a free hand in China) or they would go to war. It was reduced to a formula as simple as that.

On July 31, to pacify their German allies, who were annoyed because Japan was doing nothing to help them in their war, although she had earlier indicated that she intended to attack Russia, the Japanese government sent a message to its ambassador in Berlin, and a copy went to Admiral Nomura in Washington. This was intercepted by the Magic decoding machine and so the Americans read: "Commercial and economic relations between Japan and third countries, led by England and the United States, are gradually becoming so horribly strained that we cannot endure it much longer. Consequently, our Empire, to its very life, must take measures to secure the raw materials of the South Seas. Our Emperor must take immediate steps to break their strengthening chain of encirclement which is being woven under the guidance and with the participation of England and the United States, acting like a cunning dragon seemingly asleep. This is why we decided to obtain military bases in French Indochina and to have our troops occupy that territory . . ."

It was all there, the whole plan, as it had been decided in a series of liaison conferences between the government and military junta of Japan.

At about this time Prime Minister Konoye was making a desperate bid for a personal conference with President Roosevelt, hoping thus to cement the peace. But the Americans did not believe anything Konoye was saying, and here is why, as U.S. Secretary of War Henry L. Stimson recorded in his diary:

"They (Japanese) are trying now to get up a conference between Konoye and President Roosevelt on a most engaging program of peace while at the same time they are carrying on negotiations with their Ambassadors throughout the world showing that on its face this is a pure blind and that they have already made up their minds to a policy of going south through Indochina and Thailand."

That was not quite true, although it certainly seemed so to the Americans. What the West did not understand was that they were dealing with two entities: the Japanese government, which represented the Emperor and really wanted to make peace if they could find a way to solve their economic problems, and the military clique, which had seized control of Japan to such an extent that the government could not function if the army opposed it, because the war minister would quit, and every cabinet had to have a war minister.

So although the Americans could be pardoned for their rejection of the Japanese negotiations at this point, the negotiations were real. Only the army wanted them to fail.

In July, the Hawaiian air force prepared a staff report on air defense of the islands. It was done by Colonel William E. Farthing, commander of the 5th Bombardment Group at Hickam Field. At the request of the War Department a bit later that summer, it was amplified into what was called "The Farthing Report." It was a plan for the employment of bombardment aviation in the Defense of Oahu. The key to the plan was a provision for a complete search of the Hawaiian area daily during daylight, and an attack force available on call. The report predicted that the Japanese would employ six carriers in an attack on Hawaii, and the attack would be made early in the morning.

The solution was for the War Department to provide 180 B-17 aircraft and 36 long-range torpedo bombers.

The report closed with a warning that the attack had to be expected at anytime in the future. (This was July 1941, remember.)

The Farthing report was brilliant and perceptive and, as things turned out, it hit the nail right on the head, but there was a problem about it. Because of the attitude of the Congress about military spending in the past few years, the army had only 109 B-17 bombers available, and they were committed to Britain, the Philippines, and mainland defense, as well as Hawaii. The army decided there was no way the army could produce 180 bombers in the next few months, and so no one even tried.

Therefore, by midsummer, the analysts had it that the Japanese would attack with six carriers in the morning, and the enemy would be more interested in making a successful attack than in losses sustained. That was true too, but only at the top. It was the attitude of Admiral Yamamoto, but not the attitude of Admiral Nagumo, whose most trenchant worry was that he would lose any carriers at all. In the end, his fear was to color the whole proceedings.

But in America, among the press and public came a growing air of belligerence, indicated by a Gallup poll in September 1941, which showed that the number of people who were ready to "talk tough to Japan, even at the risk of war" had risen from 51 percent in July to 70 percent. Part of that feeling (which was certainly not shared by the military, which was fighting for time to build resources) was stirred by the newspapers. According to reports of journalists who visited Pearl Harbor, a Japanese attack was really impossible. The Japanese fleet would have no bases from which to operate and American patrols would spot them long before they arrived off Hawaii. The American navy was bursting with pride and ready for a fight, said the press, and would like nothing better than to see the Japanese fleet outside Pearl Harbor so they could blast it away.

Where the journalists got that sort of information no one said, but it could not have been from the headquarters of the Pacific Fleet, where the consciousness of unreadiness and lack of personnel and equipment was a constant worry.

General Martin planned a full-scale war game involving a pretended surprise attack by the Japanese fleet for November 17 through 22. So the army planned. The navy was having some internal difficulties, based around two areas: Naval Intelligence, where the Washington main office insisted that it should have all the information and make all the decisions and was not giving Pearl Harbor information that it needed, and the Naval War Plans Office, where Admiral Richmond Kelly Turner felt that anything to do with planning for attack or defense was his personal task, and who also was withholding information from Pearl Harbor. For example, the Japanese sent a series of messages about their routine of keeping track of the presence of ships of the American fleet in Pearl Harbor, information that was widely circulated in Washington but never got to Pearl Harbor. After the fact, when Admiral Kimmel learned of the information that had been withheld he was very bitter about it, and with more than a little reason. All the authorities were saying that the Japanese were not planning any sort of attack, and if Kimmel had known that they were watching the daily comings and goings of his ships he would have come to the obvious opposite conclusion. They were planning an attack. But not knowing, unwarned, his hands were tied.

The collapse of the Konoye cabinet on October 16, 1941, sent a flap raging through Washington, beginning with the President, who canceled a cabinet meeting of his own and conferred with his principal defense officials for two hours. The feeling that war was near permeated Washington, and even Admiral Turner prepared a message so indicating, a message that Admiral Stark, the chief of naval operations, toned down considerably because he did not really believe it.

Admiral Kimmel's reaction was swift. He alerted American submarines to be prepared to start for Japanese waters on short notice. Several other submarines were put out on war patrols to watch for an enemy fleet. Planes were dispatched to Midway to undertake daily patrols, and more were sent to Wake to do the same. Kimmel reinforced all the American bases in the Pacific — Guam, Wake, Midway, Palmyra — with ammunition and marines and planes. His cruisers and battleships were put out on alert against a possible attack.

But through all this Admiral Stark continued to believe that it was much excitement about nothing, and he so wrote to Admiral Kimmel. Also by mid-November, the Japanese fleet, knowing that it was moving its carrier unit around so much the activity would be discovered by American radio intercepts, had established a highly active system of false radio messages that were supposed to give the location of the Japanese ships, but actually were plants. This program thoroughly confused the American Office of Naval Intelligence, which was supposed to keep track of Japanese ships' movements, and so the carrier fleet went unobserved as it prepared to move up to the Kuril Islands and from there to launch its strike against Pearl Harbor.

Tokyo also confused Washington a little more by sending Ambassador Saburo Kurusu to Washington to help Admiral Nomura, on the principle that Nomura was not really a trained diplomat and they wanted no slips from inattention to diplomatic details.

By the third week of November, the Japanese fleet was anchoring in Hitokappa Bay in the Kuril Islands, preparing to leave Japanese waters. Next stop would be the launch point about 300 miles off Hawaii, for the attack on Pearl Harbor.

In Washington the Americans were grasping at straws to keep the conversations going with the Japanese, while they rushed their preparations for war. But no one, including President Roosevelt, really expected the Japanese to act. And it was the same with the people who should have known at Pearl Harbor. On November 27, Admiral Kimmel asked his plans officer, Captain C. A. McMorris, what he thought of the possibility of a Japanese attack soon.

"None, absolutely none," said Captain McMorris.

On that day, November 27, General Marshall in Washington sent a message to General Walter Short in Hawaii that was really a war warning. It

84

said that negotiations with the Japanese had collapsed for all practical purposes, so General Short was to act accordingly — really to expect anything at all any moment and to act accordingly.

And that same day Admiral Kimmel received a war warning from the navy department.

So it was apparent to everyone that war was about to begin. Where and when, those were the questions.

Chapter 6

The Attacking Force

On April 10, 1941, the Japanese had set the stage for the organization of the Pearl Harbor task force by doing something Admiral Yamamoto and other airmen of the Imperial Navy had long advocated: They organized the First Air Fleet, a change that would ultimately bring together the six carriers *Akagi*, *Kaga*, *Soryu*, *Hiryu*, *Shokaku*, and *Zuikaku*, all modern fast ships. Yamamoto's urgings had been fed by the 1940 raid of the planes of one British carrier on the Italian fleet at Taranto, which had proved beyond any doubt that aircraft were the great striking force of the fleet.

The logical commander for this First Air Fleet would have been Vice Admiral Jisaburo Ozawa, who had commanded the First Carrier Division for a time and who was one of the most vigorous proponents of Japanese air power. But Ozawa did not have the seniority for the job, and Vice Admiral Chuichi Nagumo, a highly experienced officer in battleships, cruisers, and destroyers, did have the seniority and so he got the appointment. It is doubtful if Nagumo really wanted it very much, because his feeling about carriers was the same as that of most surface sailors, that they were valuable but vulnerable. Battleship tradition had it that the battleship was the major fighting force of the fleet. The carrier, with its guns limited to antiaircraft and its flat deck, seemed to be almost a liability at sea, vulnerable to submarine attack and easily sunk by a battleship. But of course as airmen understood, the secret of a carrier's defense was carried on the carrier, the antisubmarine aircraft patrols and the combat air patrols that circled the carrier when it was at sea.

Nagumo's last sea command had been as commander of battleships in the fleet, and then he had served as president of the Naval Staff College in Tokyo, a job he left to take the aircraft carrier group command.

Nagumo and Yamamoto were not friends; they were on different sides in the navy's politics, for one thing. Yamamoto had always espoused friendship for the United States and Britain, and he had served on the naval commissions that negotiated the international naval agreements of 1930 and 1934. He believed that if Japan engaged in war with the West she would lose, and he was content to abide by the naval agreements.

Nagumo espoused the fleet theory of the navy, which was that Japan had the right to maintain the largest navy in the Pacific and should not be bound by the United States and Britain, particularly since they continued to insist on the five-five-three ratio of ships. This brought on the quarrel that caused Japan to refuse to sign the Treaty of 1934 and begin a furious program of building that had brought her navy by 1941 past the American in size and more powerful in carriers and battleships than the British Royal Navy altogether; ten times as powerful as the fleet units the British maintained in the Orient.

This quarrel within the fleet was serious enough that Yamamoto was nearly assassinated by young officers for his views. One reason he became commander of the Combined Fleet was the decision of his friends in high places to get him off to sea, to save his life. So the differences between Yamamoto and Nagumo were anything but minor, besides which Yamamoto had a very negative view of Nagumo as a fighting man; that view was reinforced when he learned that Nagumo did not like the Pearl Harbor plan from the beginning, and even as he set sail to carry out his orders did not believe in it.

Admiral Nagumo's chief of staff was Rear Admiral Kusaka, an experienced carrier commander, although as was so common in naval air forces of that period, he was not trained as an airman. But he had commanded carriers.

The genius of the First Air Division lay in its air officer, Commander Minoru Genda, the only man of the senior staff who was an airman through and through. He was the real planner of the detail of the Pearl Harbor attack.

The First Air Division and the Striking Fleet trained all spring in 1941, and by August it had achieved a high degree of skill in night as well as daylight operations. Kagoshima on the southern tip of Kyushu became the training ground for the torpedo bombers because its layout was similar to Pearl Harbor, and day and night all summer, planes roared down above the city so low that some citizens began to object, although it did them no good.

The big problem was to adjust the Japanese torpedoes to be effective in the shallow water of the Pearl Harbor lagoon, and this took endless hours of planning and testing. Another was to train pilots and bombardiers to better methods of horizontal bombing. Actually the Japanese never did have a good bombsight for horizontal bombing, and even then, with superb training and hard work, the best they could manage was one-third effectiveness, but this was a lot more than the usual rate of accuracy of Japanese bombing, which had been hardly better than two percent. Given the Japanese propensity, particularly in China, for area bombing situations, it did not make much difference. The Japanese bombardiers aimed at big cities and they usually hit something. Since their bombing was for terrorist purposes as much as for anything else, the Imperial General Headquarters neither complained nor made much attempt to change the Japanese pattern. But the Pearl Harbor attack was something else, a matter in which pinpoint accuracy was going to be important; the raid would succeed or fail in the accuracy with which the bombers could deliver bombs and torpedoes in a small area. The pilots trained at eight different air bases that spring and summer, including the Usa base, whose name could have been seen by an American as a grim joke.

The fighter pilots were going to use the newest model Zero fighters, and they had to get used to them, to carrier landings, interception and dog fighting, two planes against three, two planes against four, two planes against six. Day after day the fighter pilots flew, until Lieutenant Commander Shigeru Itaya, their training officer, was satisfied that they were doing the job as he wanted it done.

The new carrier, *Shokaku*, 29,800 tons, left the Yokosuka Naval Dockyard on August 8, 1941, and took abroad her aircraft, twelve fighters, eighteen dive-bombers, and eighteen torpedo bombers. Her air units had already been formed and were training at Usa, Oita, and Omura air bases. So were the pilots and crew of *Zuikaku*, which was being hurried to completion for the Pearl Harbor attack. She was finished on September 25, and then two new ships became the Fifth Carrier Division, the last two of the six carriers that would participate in the Pearl Harbor raid.

In August 1941, a new element was added to the Pearl Harbor raid. For some time the Japanese

Navy had been experimenting with midget submarines that weighed 46 tons and carried two torpedoes and a crew of two men. They were 76 feet
long and only 6 feet wide, a tight fit even for Japanese sailors. They had a top speed of 19 knots,
but this speed used fuel at an alarming rate. At 4
knots they had a range of 100 miles. The submarine corps was eager to test the battle qualities of
these midgets.

Yamamoto had conceived of his carrier raid
without considering the undersea forces, a matter
that was called to his attention. He agreed that
submarine participation would be useful for several reasons. First to prevent the fleet from being
surprised en route to Pearl Harbor, second for
scouting purposes, third, of course, the possibility
of participation in the attack itself.

In September, in spite of Admiral Nagumo's reluctance, the Pearl Harbor plan began to come together. The key staff officers of the First Air Fleet
were assembled by Chief of Staff Kusaka and
briefed officially for the first time on the mission
they were going to perform. This was the meeting
at which Commander Genda was put in charge of
the problem solving: how to fuel at sea, communications, intelligence about the enemy's actions,
navigation, all the detail to be massed for an operation so unusual that the Americans did not really
believe the Japanese would ever try it. So the spe-
cialists were assembled and given tasks, such as
the method of communication when the ships
were at sea.

Commander Genda set as his first task the decision on the route to be taken to get to Hawaii. He could not make that decision — it was Nagumo's to make — but he could give all the detail, and he did for three routes, southern, central, and north.

If they went south they would leave from Hashirajima in the Inland Sea or from Saeki in northern Kyushu, then head for Wotje in the Marshall Islands, where they would refuel. They could then go east of Johnston Atoll to a point 200 to 250 miles south of Hawaii and launch the planes to attack.

It would be fine weather, and that was one of the objections: there would be no cover for the fleet from the weather. And the Americans used this area of the Pacific south of Hawaii for training, so the chances of their being discovered were great.

The second route would pass 400 miles south of Christmas Island, and then approach south of the big island of Hawaii. This plan had all the disadvantages of the other, Genda believed. The real advantage was that the Americans would never expect the Japanese to be coming at them from south of Hawaii.

If they chose the central route, they would leave from Hashirajima, rendezvous at Chichi Jima, 1,700 miles south of Tokyo. That was not a good harbor and not all the ships of the task force could fit inside. The ships would then move 500 miles north of Midway and then up to the north of Oahu, and then head south.

All this done, Genda then outlined the route by which he wanted the ships to attack, the northern route. The fleet would move through the rough northern Pacific south of the route followed by most merchant ships, so that detection would be unlikely. The ships would sail east from Hokkaido along the forty-second parallel and about 1,000 miles dead north of Oahu would turn south. This plan appealed to Genda because he said it offered the most concealment, and least chance of being detected by the American patrols.

Admiral Kusaka liked the northern approach, but Admiral Nagumo was the man who had to be convinced. Nagumo did not like it at all because of the difficulties in fueling at sea in rough weather that he knew they would have to face.

The real advantage of the northern route in Genda's eyes was the element of surprise that it offered. To Genda surprise was the key element of the whole operation. If they surprised the Americans, they could be totally successful. If they instead were surprised, all might be lost, including six carriers and all their planes.

Nagumo was very low on that concept. He did not believe it possible to surprise the Americans. He expected their presence to be discovered well before they launched the attack. He liked the southern route, with its approached to the Marshall Islands, the leisurely fueling in the protected waters there. That was the important element. Surprise — why they could not achieve surprise anyhow, so why try?

The matter hung in abeyance.

On August 15, the Navy had issued orders to the fleet to prepare for war. That meant all the training programs had to be finished up and the fleet put on a war readiness basis by October 1. Training operations in China were discontinued, and on September 1, Admiral Yamamoto issued an order for complete war organization. In September came the tabletop war games in Tokyo at the Naval Staff college, and all the problems brought out there. Nagumo kept complaining about the northern approach. In the end Nagumo was simply overpowered by everybody else and never stopped complaining about the northern route, although he grudgingly agreed that it had to be taken.

October 2 was the day that Admiral Nagumo summoned the senior officers of the First Air Fleet aboard the carrier *Kaga* for a meeting. It lasted two hours. When it was over, the men who ran the ships knew where they were going and what they were going to do. After the meeting the training increased in tempo. The Type 97 bombers would be used both for torpedo bombing and high-level horizontal bombing. And for the crews that would undertake the torpedoing of the battleships at Pearl Harbor there was final talk that it was a real test.

They were now to learn how to use torpedoes in very shallow water. They would climb to 2,000 meters and fly over the eastern tip of the volcano Sakurajima that stuck out in Kagoshima Bay, then down the valley of the Kotsuka River. The planes would be at 500-meter intervals. They would go down to 50 meters altitude, flying down the valley toward Kagoshima, and fly over the city of Kagoshima at 40 meters. After they passed over the Yamagataya Department Store on the port side they would see a large water tank on the shore. At they passed over they would drop down to 20 meters and release a torpedo. The target would be 500 meters from the shore. After they released, at 160 knots, they would fly straight, then climb to starboard and return to base. They must be very careful. At these altitudes even the slightest error could mean disaster.

The pilots of the Second Carrier Division trained at Kasanohara near Kanoya air base using the battleship *Settsu*, an ancient hulk moored in Ariake Bay, as a target for the dive-bombers. They used bombs that emitted white smoke when they made a hit. After much practice the pilots decided it would be a fine idea to delay release of their bombs, not releasing them from 600 meters but instead from 450 meters. The chances of getting a hit would be increased, they said. This matter was discussed and discussed, but as were many other things that fall, it was left in abeyance.

One of the matters to which Admiral Nagano, the chief of staff, had addressed himself was the preservation of other air units against the cannibalization by Yamamoto, but it happened anyhow. The Pearl Harbor mission diverted crews from the Third and Fourth Carrier Divisions, and particularly Zero pilots. The Third and Fourth Carrier Groups were left almost denuded of fighter pilots. And the Yokosuka Air Group was also cannibalized, to the extent that the numbers of instructors at the school had to be reduced.

Generally speaking the naval air arm was opposed to the whole Pearl Harbor operation, because they saw it taking their very best people and leaving them in trouble for the start of southern operations. The Eleventh Air Fleet was supposed to cover the operations in the Philippines and so a new generation of fighter pilots had to be trained in a hurry. The Third and Fourth Carrier Division were to be employed in the Philippines and the south, and they were awfully short of trained pilots. But there was nothing to be done. Yamamoto had gathered a head of steam, and he was going to have his way.

In early October some hard decisions had to be made. Vice Admiral Gunichi Mikawa, the commander of Battleship Division Three, wanted to take all four of his battleships to Pearl Harbor, but Admiral Yamamoto said no, only two would go. The others were needed for the southern operation.

Admiral Nobutake Kondo, commander of the southern operation, wanted more air power and was highly skeptical of the whole Hawaii plan. But Yamamoto persisted and promised Kondo that he would have the use of the six carriers from Hawaii just as soon as the operation ended. He said nothing of his feeling that they might well lose half the carriers at Pearl Harbor.

What about the midget submarines? Yamamoto was willing that they should go, if the submarine force could solve the technical problems. The submarine force said it could, and so the decks of the big submarines were prepared to take on the midgets.

On October 12, after meetings abroad the flagship *Nagato* all day, the senior commander stayed for supper and had a party to note the end of maneuvers. The next day, October 13, Yamamoto held an informal meeting at which all the senior officers were invited to state their views on the coming attack — and almost all of them turned out to be against it. It was too far, the element of surprise would be missing because the negotiations with the Americans were already breaking down and the Americans would be preparing for war. It was too late in the year and the weather would not be right. Every conceivable negative argument was brought out again. Yamamoto heard them all out, and then he spoke. He took cognizance of all the negatives, and then he said, loud and clear:

"So long as I am commander in chief of the Combined Fleet," he said, "Pearl Harbor will be attacked. I ask you to give me your fullest support. Return to your stations and work hard for the success of Japan's war plan. Good luck."

Admiral Nagumo's negative attitude was a source of much concern to Yamamoto. Yamamoto's chief of staff, Vice Admiral Matome Ugaki, suggested that Nagumo really should either step out of the operation or be pushed out, given his feeling that it would not be successful and the way he dragged his feet all the way. Yamamoto considered it and he could have done it, but there was no other candidate for the job who would be any better. Admiral Ozawa, the logical choice, had been appointed to lead the south seas attack, which was really more important to the Japanese Navy, at least in the short run, because it meant control of the Dutch oil resources. So there was no logical alternative to Nagumo, and much as Yamamoto did not like it, he decided to swallow his distaste and hope for the best.

By mid-October Admiral Kusaka had worked out the fueling system, so that the fleet could fuel at sea. First, when the fleet set out for Hawaii, every fuel tank would be full, and fuel containers would be put in every cranny. Special permission to do this was needed from the Naval Affairs Bureau, but it was obtained. The destroyers did not have much fuel capacity and on the trip to Hawaii they would have to fuel every day. That could not be helped. It could not even be worried about, because there was so much else to worry over.

Those special shallow-water torpedoes had been projected by the torpedo plan, but they were not delivered by the end of October. Commander Fuchida and others connected with the air strike began to have dreadful visions of torpedoes that did not come at all.

But the torpedoes finally arrived and were stowed aboard the ships and another crisis was averted.

On October 29 Admiral Tomioka of the Naval General Staff came to visit the flagship *Nagato*, to announce that the General Staff had accepted the Yamamoto plan and put it in the war orders. Now Tokyo wanted a date for the attack, and it was settled that it would be on December 7 Hawaii time or December 8 Tokyo time. The date was fixed because of several factors. The Japanese were aware of the Americans' speedup in defense operations and could see that the United States was becoming stronger every day. They knew that in later December the Pacific weather grew ferocious and remained that way until March. They knew that they were eating rapidly into their stockpile of fuel, more rapidly even than they had feared. The moon would be proper in this period for night operations, particularly in the south. The army wanted to move to avoid the worst of the monsoon season, and finally the Japanese knew that the United States Pacific Fleet's schedule of operations meant that almost every Saturday night and Sunday morning the fleet was in port.

The decision was made and ratified, first at a liaison conference between government and military men, and then at an Imperial conference.

On November 2, all the ships that would participate in the Pearl Harbor attack were gathered in Ariake Bay, and the next day Admiral Nagumo informed the ship captains of what they were

going to do. On November 3, Commander
Fuchida staged a practice "raid," and that afternoon they held a critique. There would not be
time for many more such practices. Time was
growing very short. Admiral Yamamoto came to
the *Akagi* on the afternoon of November 4, fresh
from a visit to Tokyo where many decisions had
been made, especially the one that December 1
was the point of no return. But he had promised
to call back Nagumo's task force if the negotiations with America succeeded at the last minute,
except that the last minute had to be December 1.
After that it was too late or it might be too late. It
would be "in the lap of the gods," Yamamoto
said.

While in Tokyo, Yamamoto had his chance to
get rid of Nagumo and did not. Admiral Shimada,
the Minister of the Navy, asked him if he wanted
to make any changes in the command structures.
But Yamamoto felt it would be worse and more
difficult at this stage to change Nagumo than to
put up with him, for at least Kusaka, his chief of
staff, had come around to supporting the Pearl
Harbor plan and had added several dimensions to
it. So the chance passed, and whatever happened
now, Yamamoto would have to live with in the
knowledge that he had so ordered.

The second "dress rehearsal" for the Pearl
Harbor attack came on November 5. It ended
successfully at midday, although the attackers had
been spotted by the Americans and had been engaged in a lengthy air battle before getting to the

target. The one trouble that bothered Commander Fuchida most was that the torpedoes were running too deep. This must be adjusted. It would never do if it lasted until Pearl Harbor. The whole mission could fail.

On November 7, Admiral Ugaki was working on the 100-page Combined Fleet Operational Order No. 1. Meanwhile the fliers worked on the torpedo problem, which they solved by November 13, and achieved 82 percent hits in their latest trial. The airmen heaved great sighs of relief.

On November 9, *Shokaku* and *Zuikaku* stopped at Kure and *Akagi* and *Kaga* went to Sasebo. At these ports all the unnecessary items were unloaded from each vessel, everything to make room for extra fuel. Admiral Nagumo, in turn, issued Striking Force Operations Order No. 1: The force would complete battle preparations by November 20 and assemble at Hitokappu Bay in the Kuril Islands.

Vice Admiral Mitsumi Shimizu's submarines were also now informed that they were going to take part. It came as a huge shock to Captain Sasaki, commander of the First Submarine Division, when he was told to go to Kure and get his submarines, which had been undergoing modifications. Only then did he learn that he was supposed to carry midget submarines, about which he knew nothing, not even if the deck of his submarines would support their weight. Admiral

Shimizu put together his operational plan, which included scouting Lahaina roads on Maui, where elements of the fleet sometimes visited, the Aleutians, and some points in the South Pacific. His twenty-five submarines, five of them carrying midgets, would surround Oahu and release their midgets, which would go into Pearl Harbor. If the ships came out, the submarines would be waiting for them.

On November 11, the Third Submarine Squadron sailed from Saeki Bay for Pearl Harbor by way of Kwajalein in the Marshall Islands.

On the morning of November 12, Admiral Yamamoto and Admiral Ugaki left Tokyo by train for Yokosuka, and soon they were aboard the *Nagato*. A final conference of leaders of the Pearl Harbor mission was held on November 13. Two days later Yamamoto and Ugaki were working on army-navy agreements for the whole war effort.

Admiral Shimizu did not much like the whole midget submarine idea. He wondered how he was going to rescue the crews of the midgets from Pearl Harbor. But when he visited the midget base at Kure and met the crews, he was impressed by their exaltation and air of self-sacrifice. They were not worrying about being rescued. They were worrying about getting inside the harbor and torpedoing ships. Now the action increased in tempo.

November 13. The *Akagi* hoisted anchor and sailed off the coast of Kagoshima, where her planes and flying officers came abroad. On November 14, she moved into Saeki Bay, where Nagumo and his staff boarded the ship.

November 15. The leaders of the army, the navy, and the government gathered at the Imperial Palace to brief Emperor Hirohito on the forthcoming Southern Operation and Pearl Harbor raid. In fact, however, Pearl Harbor was the last of it. The really important matter was that Japan was preparing to move into Malaya, the Philippines, Hong Kong, and thence to the Dutch East Indies. Virtually no time was spent explaining Pearl Harbor, for there was no need; the Emperor had known about the Yamamoto plan for a long time.

November 16. The *Shokaku* sailed from Kure to Beppu to pick up her planes and crews. So did the *Soryu*.

November 17. The *Zuikaku* picked up her crew. So did the *Hiryu*. It was necessary to conceal all this movement from the Japanese people and neutrals, who might have big mouths and big ears and eyes. So as the carrier planes left the fields, planes of the Twelfth Combined Naval Air Corps landed there and apparently all the training flights went on as before.

The carriers and the aircraft exchanged messages as they had been doing, and to the Americans listening from abroad, there was no indication of any unusual carrier activity in these hectic days.

November 17. The *Nagato* arrived at Saeki Bay and Admiral Yamamoto went to the *Akagi* to address the key officers of the First Air Fleet. About 100 assembled on the flight deck to hear Yamamoto, who spoke extemporaneously and from the heart. He spoke of Admiral Kimmel, for whom he had such great respect. He spoke of the American Navy, which might well rise up and smite them. They had to expect that possibility. He spoke of the Japanese fighting man's tradition, not the fake *bushido* of the army, but the real thing of his own *samurai* family. "It is the custom of *bushido* to select an equal or stronger opponent," he said. "On this score you have nothing to complain about. The American Navy is a good match for the Japanese Navy."

In the wardroom of the carrier there was a farewell party. They ate dried cuttlefish for happiness and walnuts for victory and then drank a toast to the Emperor and to the coming battle.

Late that afternoon *Soryu* and *Hiryu* with four destroyers left Saeki Bay for the Kurils. That evening, one by one, the ships sailed, in twos and threes, training all the way.

That night *Shokaku* sailed, and then *Zuikaku* and *Akagi*, still blacked out in the bay, weighed anchor and moved quietly out to sea with two detours.

All evening as his striking force went out, Admiral Yamamoto stood on the deck of the flagship *Nagato* and watched, until darkness was complete and even with night glasses he could see no more.

November 18. Morning. The submarines with

their five midgets left Kure and began the long journey to Pearl Harbor.

November 19. The *I-26* sailed from Yokosuka to scout in northern waters, especially the Aleutians. She was to watch for any sort of American activity.

November 20. The Japanese-American negotiations continued in Washington. They seemed to be at an impasse but everybody hoped. The Japanese presented a new proposition. The Americans called it preposterous — the Japanese demanded all the oil they wanted in exchange for a Japanese commitment not to attack anywhere. Oh yes, the Americans would also have to abandon Chiang Kai-shek.

November 22. All the Japanese ships of the Hawaii Striking Force had arrived in Hitokappu Bay. Admiral Nagumo held an intelligence briefing at which the disposition and all new information about the American fleet were revealed.

November 23. A special conference was called by Admiral Nagumo aboard the *Akagi*. For the first time all the ship captains learned that their mission was to attack Pearl Harbor. The whole plan was revealed with the caveat that if by some miracle, agreement could be reached in Washington, the whole attack was off. All day long Fuchida gave smaller briefings, to his airmen particularly. For now they were about to sever their connection with Japan. There would be no more information for them unless it was emergency information. Everything had now to be primed for the big day of the attack.

November 26. A cold and unfriendly day in the north sea of Hitokappu. The striking force started out one by one. They sailed. They did not know what they were going to meet, how many carriers the Americans had, and whether or not they could make the surprise attack they felt was so necessary for their success. Admiral Nagumo remained apprehensive; what if they did not surprise the Americans but ran into a surprise themselves? He felt, and Yamamoto admitted, that this whole adventure was a desperate gamble that could end in victory or disaster. And who knew which?

Chapter 7

December 6 — At Sea

The Japanese attack force slipped out of Hitokappu Bay and headed for Pearl Harbor in gray and wintry weather, low clouds hanging from a leaden sky, and the men who had to venture onto the decks of the ships were pelted with snow. At least they had every assurance that the Naval General Staff in Tokyo could give them that they were not likely to be surprised en route to Hawaii. A month earlier, Naval Intelligence had sent the merchant ship *Taiyo Maru* sailing from Yokohama, ostensibly to pick up any Japanese citizens in Hawaii and on the West Coast of America who wanted to return home in these difficult times between the nations. Actually the *Taiyo Maru* was on an espionage mission, carrying three naval officers — Commander Toshihide Maejima, Sublieutenant Keio Matsuo, both submariners who were to get information that would be valuable for the midget submarines, and Lt. Commander

Suguru Suzuki, an aviation officer.

On the voyage to Hawaii, following the route the striking force would take, they made careful weather observations and kept careful records. They also watched constantly for ships to see if any American warships were moving about these waters. When the *Taiyo Maru* was 100 miles north of Oahu they did see a formation of American planes, and Suzuki noted that this could be the attack line, the point beyond which the Americans would not be patrolling.

When they got to Hawaii they summed up the results. The weather all the way across had been fine, except for one storm. They had sighted no patrol craft north of Midway, and reconnaissance north of Oahu could not extend more than 200 miles. They had not sighted a single vessel on the whole voyage.

The *Taiyo Maru* entered Honolulu Harbor on Saturday morning, November 1. They were coming in on the weekend, and could see what it would be like for Admiral Nagumo a few weeks in the future.

These officers did not go ashore because they did not want to attract attention. Instead they set up a telephone line from the bridge of the ship to the gangway on the dock. Several members of the Japanese consulate staff came to the dock as was quite natural, and they conferred with the naval officers over this telephone. Consul Nagano Kita came aboard and conferred with Suzuki. They asked for and got all the information the consular staff had on the American fleet. They observed all the army and navy patrol flights that flew around Hawaii, types and number of aircraft, and their formations.

On November 5, the *Taiyo Maru* left Honolulu again and headed back to Japan. She was the last Japanese ship to call at that Hawaii port.

As the Japanese ships began to assemble at Hitokappu Bay, the *Taiyo Maru* reached Japan having taken the route home that Admiral Nagumo would use. They saw that air patrols were weak in the north and west, that there were no planes in the Midway skies, that they saw no ships on the voyage.

When the ship reached Japan the naval officers were whisked off and driven swiftly to Tokyo. They were to report that afternoon to the Naval General Staff.

At two o'clock in the afternoon they went to a room in the Navy Ministry. Admiral Nagano was there, as well as Fukudome and Tomioka and many important people from the staff and operations and from intelligence. Lt. Commander Suzuki reported first; the admirals were visibly impressed and relieved to hear that the American air patrols were weak. But one question Suzuki could not answer. What were the Americans doing with their carriers? Because they did not seem to be operating with the fleet, their times of entry and departure varied so.

After the briefing, Lt. Commander Suzuki then prepared to go to Hitokappu Bay to brief Admiral

Nagumo and his staff before they set out on the long voyage. His description of the unreadiness of the Americans seemed to calm Admiral Nagumo's nerves.

Admiral Nagumo's flagship led nine new destroyers, the two battleships *Hiei* and *Kirishima* and the heavy cruisers *Tone* and *Chikuma*. The six carriers would not make any air patrols on the voyage, they would depend for information on the submarine fleet and particularly three very large submarines that carried aircraft.

The submarine force carrying the Special Attack (Midget) Submarines had sailed from Kure on November 18. Before they sailed the men heard a message from Vice Admiral Shimizu, commander of the Sixth Fleet.

"Now listen carefully," Shimizu had said, "X-day, the day to open hostilities, is set for December 8; the time daybreak. The order to open fire will be issued by the General Staff of the navy in Tokyo, just before the time set for the attack. Under no circumstances are you to take action unless ordered."

The submarines sailed at noon and by evening had reached Nasaka Jima, a small island on the Inland Sea. The next stop would be Pearl Harbor. On November 19, they sailed for Pearl Harbor.

The crew of one of the midget submarines consisted of Ensign Kazuo Sakamaki and a petty officer, carried by the *I-24*. Every day on the voyage they went into their midget submarine lashed to the deck and worked out navigational problems for the Pearl Harbor area.

The Japanese force headed eastward through heavy seas. During the first half of the cruise a quarter of the men on the ships manned their battle stations, and a lookout scanned the seas twenty-four hours a day, keeping a sharp eye out for what they feared most, the periscope of an American submarine. Aboard each of the six carriers six fighter planes were ready day and night and six pilots were in the ready room, prepared to man the planes if anyone challenged the fleet on its way.

For the Japanese fliers, training continued daily, approach to the target, ship and plane recognition, and study of the scale models of Oahu and Pearl Harbor. At night the ships closed formation and the three big submarines clustered around the *Akagi*, the carrier flagship. The blackout was observed strictly and radio silence kept the ships as quiet as if they had been sailing vessels.

On November 30, the night came in foggy and wet, and throughout it the Japanese ships used their searchlights to keep together. In the daylight hours they moved out again.

A long way ahead of the attack fleet, the submarine *I-26*, which had left Japan on November 19, moved to the Aleutian Islands, and on November 26 it was in the Kiska area. The submarine's captain checked Kiska and found no activity there worthy of note, then sailed for Adak Strait. Once more the findings were negative. On November

29, the *I-26* was off Dutch Harbor. Again no sign of any American naval vessels was observed, so the I-boat headed out to sea.

The scouting submarine *I-10* launched its aircraft for a night flight over Suva bay in the Fiji Islands. The plane flew over the harbor, saw nothing, and reported to the submarine. Then the plane disappeared. The submarine waited and searched for three days, but the plane had vanished. So the first blood of the attack had been shed.

Every day the Japanese destroyers refueled, but even so to save fuel the ships were completely unheated, and the use of electric lights was kept to a minimum. On most of the ships the crew and officers washed in cold water.

In Tokyo the tension grew day by day and hour by hour as the army and navy high commands waited for the fateful moment, the hour of the attack on Pearl Harbor, which would also symbolize the whole southern operations and the war. Admiral Yamamoto journeyed from his flagship on the afternoon of December 1, for he had been summoned for an audience with the Emperor on December 2. It was the Imperial pleasure to grant an audience to top military commanders on the eve of war, a practice begun by Hirohito's grandfather. That afternoon of December 1, the cabinet and military leaders held their last prewar imperial conference in the East Room of the Palace, where they had been meeting in recent months to symbolize the oneness of government and the Imperial throne in all matters. Prime Minister Tojo was very grave and very tired. He spoke of the possibility of a long war but said he hoped for a short one. The Emperor listened, smiled, and left the room before the others. He seemed to be in excellent spirits. He had accommodated himself to the prospect, which only two days earlier had left him worried and doubting.

For months, the Emperor had lectured the military and political leaders on the need to use every effort to resolve Japan's difficulties with America without resorting to war. On September 6, a fateful Imperial conference had been held at which the military leaders and Prince Konoye had apparently agreed that war was the only answer. Then Konoye, a month later, had given up trying to forestall war and quit. The Emperor had then appointed General Tojo to form a cabinet, on the principle that Tojo was the only general known at the Imperial Palace who might control the generals and avoid war. The Emperor had told Tojo when he appointed him to forget the September 6 decision as if it had never been made, and to start all over again with diplomatic means to settle the differences, and Tojo had promised to do so.

It had also been well known around the palace that Admiral Yamamoto and other admirals did not want war with America. But on November 30, Prince Takamatsu, the emperor's younger brother, had come to see Hirohito. He had joined the navy and had been appointed to the operations section of the Naval General Staff. At the office he had learned that the navy had been preparing for war with America for many months.

When Hirohito heard this he was shocked and upset. He had been told the contrary. So what was he to believe? What was he to believe about the "honest efforts" of any of his admirals or generals to avoid war? That day, November 30, Hirohito had called for the Marquis Kido, his closest adviser in recent months, and had told him he was upset. Kido had suggested that the Emperor call in Admiral Shimada, the navy minister, and Admiral Nagano, the navy chief of staff, and find out the facts from them. Hirohito did call in these officers that day and he questioned them. They said that the navy generally had not wanted war. That the navy did not believe that Japan should fight America or that Japan could beat America. "But," said the two admirals, "we are better prepared for fighting now than we will be a year from now."

They seemed to share Admiral Yamamoto's feeling that if Japan was very lucky she could strike some serious blows, and then offer peace, keeping her gains and particularly settling the China matter with America. They were convinced that the Western world was closing in around them and that this was a last chance.

The statements of the admirals seemed to have settled Hirohito's mind, and the next day at the Imperial conference, he seemed confident for the future, which heartened all his officers.

On December 2, the submarines that would ring Hawaii at the time of the attack left Truk Island for Kwajalein. From Kwajalein Admiral Shimizu would direct the submarine operations. By this time, Admiral Nagumo's force had covered about half the distance to Hawaii. Still radio silence was kept, the fleet getting its weather reports from blind broadcasts made in code by Tokyo every hour on the hour. But there was no indication on the airwaves that a Japanese naval force was at sea.

Admiral Shigeyoshi Inoue's Fourth Fleet was en route to the Bonin Islands, and in three days it would head for Guam, which was to be one of the points of capture in the opening days of war. Admiral Kondo's Second Fleet was in the Pescadores, and would sail in a few hours for the south. The fleet's job was to escort the troops and pave the way for the invasion of the Philippines, Malaya, and then the Dutch East Indies, and to prepare for the invasion of Timor and Burma.

Admiral Ozawa was on his way to Hainan to escort the army force of General Tomoyuke Yamashita in its trip to Thailand and Malaya, which would be the attack on Malaya. Admiral Korekiyu Takahashi's southern invasion force was also in the Pescadores, waiting for X-Day, when it would begin the invasion of the Philippines with 100 vessels. And Admiral Takeo Takagi led his Philippines Support Force to Palau, 500 miles east of the southern Philippines. He, too, was waiting for X-Day.

But everything waited for Nagumo. His signal that he had attacked Pearl Harbor would bring all these other forces into motion. And if the signal were not given, then nothing would happen.

On December 2, the word flashed to Yamamoto's flagship from the Imperial Naval Staff in Tokyo. The decision for war had been affirmed. The date and time would be ordered later.

Admiral Ugaki, Yamamoto's chief of staff, radioed (in code) all the fleets at sea and gave them the word. Now Admiral Nagumo knew that only an eleventh-hour callback, which signaled success in the diplomatic negotiations in Washington, could prevent the Pearl Harbor attack. Given the attitudes of the two parties, both belligerent, there was really no chance that such agreements could be reached.

On December 2, the Japanese foreign office sent messages to all its consuls and diplomats in North America, the Philippines, Canada, Panama, Cuba, the South Seas, British, and Dutch Territory to destroy their codebooks and secret documents, but to do it quietly so as not to arouse any suspicions.

Also on December 2, the Japanese foreign office outposts in London, Hong Kong, Singapore, and Manila reported that they had disposed of their Purple coding machines. The Americans at Pearl Harbor refused to put any special emphasis on this, because they knew that the Japanese destroyed their codes from time to time. But Naval Intelligence in Washington and the War Plans division in Washington were so closely guarding the secrets they possessed that Admiral Kimmel did not even know what a Purple machine was or the significance of its destruction. By this time, in many ways it was quite apparent that Washington was withholding all sorts of vital information from Admiral Kimmel's command, playing the old Washington game of naval power politics as usual.

On December 4, Admiral Nagumo's striking force ran into rough seas. So the destroyer refueling was canceled for the day. The Japanese had crossed the international dateline and had changed over to Hawaii time.

On December 5, the mother submarine that was carrying Ensign Sakamaki's midget submarine came into Hawaiian waters, and the radio operator tuned in to a Hawaiian radio station. That day Ensign Sakamaki discovered that the gyrocompass of his submarine was not working. Without it his chance of succeeding in navigating to the target were minimal.

At 11:30 on December 6 Admiral Nagumo's striking force changed course, swinging to 180 degrees, toward Hawaii and increasing speed to 20 knots. A few minutes later the flagship *Akagi* hoisted a historic flag, the one used by Admiral Togo at the Battle of Tsushima when he defeated the Russian Baltic Fleet. Admiral Yamamoto's final message was signaled through the fleet:

"The rise and fall of the Emperor depends upon this battle. Every man will do his duty."

At 3:00 P.M. on December 6, Takeo Yoshikawa, a Japanese naval intelligence officer who had been sent to Honolulu a month earlier to spy on the American fleet, set out for his last check on the position of the ships. He rode in a taxicab and no one paid any attention to him at Aiea and the Pearl City pier from which he had a good view of the harbor and Ford Island. He then went back to the consulate and prepared a detailed message for Tokyo, telling of the fleet disposition and the fact that there appeared to be no aerial reconnaissance around the island. It ended:

"On the evening of December 5, the *Utah* and a seaplane tender entered the harbor. Ships in port on December 6 are nine battleships, three light cruisers, and two destroyers in the docks. All heavy cruisers and carriers are out of the harbor."

Then Yoshikawa used a special code prepared by a German agent who was also a Japanese agent at Hawaii, since the Purple machine had already been destroyed.

That German agent was Dr. Bernard Julius Otto Kuehn, who in 1928 had become a member of the German Navy's secret police. He had joined the Nazi party in 1930. In 1935 he had made contact with the Japanese naval attaché in Berlin and had been employed by the Japanese as an espionage agent in Hawaii, under a contract for two years, with a salary of $2,000 a month plus an annual bonus of $6,000. The contract had been renewed time and again, and Kuehn had functioned as a Japanese agent, with his contacts at the Japanese consulate in Honolulu. He had been living in Hawaii since 1936, where he said he was a student of Japanese at the University of Hawaii. His wife and family were with him. In 1935 and 1936, he had visited Japan for instructions. In 1939 a Japanese intelligence officer had come to Hawaii and given him a radio transmitter and told him to go underground. If war came between the United States and Japan, Kuehn was to use the radio to make contact with Japanese submarines off the Hawaii coast.

In 1941, several contacts were made with Kuehn, as Japanese naval intelligence prepared for the war. Some $14,000 was delivered to him one day. He was also again told to lie low, and be prepared to establish an intelligence ring after the war began, when it was anticipated that all the Japanese consulate staff would be picked up.

So the Yoshikawa message was put into Kuehn's code and sent. After Yoshikawa had reported that the carriers were not at Pearl Harbor, Nagumo and his staff had hoped they would find them at Lahaina, on Maui, but that night the submarine *I-72* reported there were no warships at Lahaina.

Where were the American carriers? That became Admiral Nagumo's greatest worry — he might yet be surprised by the Americans.

Commander Genda, the planner of the air strikes, napped in the operations room of the *Akagi* from 8:00 to 10:00 P.M. Then he went up to the flight deck to watch the mechanics making the first attack wave ready for action. Commander Fuchida, who would direct the attack from the air, stopped in the wardroom for conversation with some of his fliers. He advised them to get to bed and get some sleep. He went to his own cabin at 10:00 P.M. and went to bed. At 10:50 on the night of December 6, Ensign Sakamaki looked through the periscope of the mother submarine and saw the red and green lights of Pearl Harbor 20 miles away. The submarine captain showed him the message from Admiral Yamamoto ordering the attack. The captain asked Sakamaki what he wanted to do, go on with the mission or abort because of the faulty gyrocompass?

"Captain, I am going ahead," said the ensign.

"On to Pearl Harbor!" said the captain.

Ensign Sakamaki then entered his midget submarine and his petty officer joined him. It was almost 11:00 P.M., the night of December 6. Ten miles south of Pearl Harbor the midget submarine was released. So were all the other four. The Striking Force was now traveling at 24 knots on its way to Hawaii, the cruiser *Abukuma* leading, four destroyers behind her, then the two battleships in a column, with the two heavy cruisers to port and starboard, and the six carriers in two parallel columns behind. The carriers were flanked by destroyers and destroyers brought up the rear of the force. The destination was a point 200 miles north of Oahu, to be reached before dawn.

Chapter 8

The Problem of Readiness

The conventional wisdom of the 1940s and 1950s held that Admiral Husband E. Kimmel and Lt. General Short were surprised by the Japanese on December 7, 1941, because they were less than competent in organizing their defenses. Because of this attitude, their careers were blasted, and the navy, at least, lost one of its most talented commanders.

But since those days, when Congress demanded scalps, and the navy gave them the whole heads of General Short and Admiral Kimmel, new evidence has come to hand to prove quite a different case.

Admiral Kimmel, who was really the man entrusted with the air defense of Pearl Harbor and Oahu because the navy had the only large supply of patrol bombers, was the victim of Washington naval politics in which a handful of key officials were using the intelligence they gained about

Japanese activity for their personal purposes, to gain recognition and importance. Washington, not the Pacific Fleet command at Pearl Harbor, was responsible for the surprise of the American forces. Kimmel was systematically deprived of vital information about Japanese intentions and operations that would have made it possible for him to mount the air searches that would have led to a discovery of the Japanese fleet approaching from the north of Hawaii, long before the Japanese could have launched their aircraft. The result of the battle might not have been so dissimilar. The Japanese had 6 carriers in action. The army air forces had only 137 planes on Oahu, only 6 of them B-17 bombers in service, and there was not a single American carrier in the immediate vicinity, but at least Admiral William F. Halsey's task force could have arrived and the American aircraft in Hawaii would have been alerted and ready to fight rather than blasted like so many clay pigeons on the ground. Also the battle fleet would have been able to get up steam and escape from the narrow confines of Pearl Harbor and most of the ships probably would have survived intact.

A major failure in the Washington planning for months beforehand was the refusal of the American military establishment to send an adequate number of aircraft to the defense of Hawaii. This decision was made because no one in Washington believed that the Japanese would really stage an air strike across the Pacific Ocean against this formidable naval base. The conventional wisdom said that it could not possibly occur because it could not possibly succeed. This attitude was as widely held in Japan as it was in the United States and accounts for the fact that Admiral Yamamoto did not actually receive the go-ahead from Naval Headquarters in Tokyo, although he had made all the plans and preparations and threatened to resign his post if the navy did not go along, until just a few days before the launching of the attack from the Kuril Islands.

One important aspect of the failure of the Americans to realize what was coming was the orientation of the defense community in Washington. Almost all eyes were turned to the Atlantic where the U-boat menace was very severe that fall of 1941.

Another part of the problem was the breakdown of the intelligence processes in Washington because of the personal ambitions of several officers.

The fact was that over the summer months the Japanese had sent out many clues, which were either misinterpreted by the American intelligence community or ignored. Ignoring arose because the American naval command had decided that it was impossible for the Japanese to attack Pearl Harbor. First of all it meant maintaining total secrecy all the time the attack force was crossing the Pacific, and no one thought this was possible, and in this they joined the Japanese Naval General

Staff, which called Yamamoto's plan suicidal nonsense.

So, since there could not possibly be an attack on Pearl Harbor the U.S. Navy was free to turn its eyes elsewhere. Only Admiral Kimmel's command at Pearl Harbor was concerned. The plans officer had also decided that an air attack was most unlikely. But more important than such thoughts was the overriding deficiency: the Pacific Fleet did not have much information about what the Japanese were up to. It was withheld by Washington. And even though Washington knew by early December that Japanese fleets were at sea, heading for southeast points, the same information was withheld from General MacArthur and Asiatic Fleet Commander Admiral Thomas C. Hart. So that when the Japanese arrived on December 8, almost half a day after the Pearl Harbor attack, the American B-17s on Luzon airfields were destroyed before they could get off the ground.

For more than ten years the Americans had been breaking the Japanese naval and diplomatic codes. The information had become scantier since 1940 when the Japanese changed several of their codes, and the American code breakers were playing catch-up.

And for almost a year Admiral Kimmel had been struggling to prevent the decimation of his forces by Washington, which wanted to use part of the Pacific Fleet to shore up the Atlantic operations. Only President Roosevelt's refusal to remove very many ships from the fleet had saved it from the chief of naval operations, Admiral Stark.

In the spring of 1941, the pressure was again on the Pacific Fleet, this time because Washington was paying too much attention to the negotiations being conducted by Admiral Nomura, the Japanese ambassador in Washington. Nomura was a man of peace, although he was an admiral. He believed thoroughly in a peaceful settlement of the differences between the United States and Japan. That is why he was sent to Washington, but the cynicism behind his dispatch was complete. Because he believed in what he was doing, the Japanese government knew that he would be persuasive. Meanwhile the army and navy prepared unstintingly for war. At the proper time Nomura would be sacrificed. And now on the eve of the attack against Pearl Harbor the time had almost arrived.

Since the Americans were reading all the dispatches Nomura sent and received, they knew that Nomura was sincere in his approaches to them. Thus the navy and political chiefs of the United States concluded that there could be no Japanese attack while the negotiations continued. They forgot completely the events of February 1904, when the Japanese fleet attacked the Russian squadron at Port Arthur without warning, thus opening the Russo-Japanese War.

Early in the spring of 1941 Admiral Turner, the navy chief of war plans, had been so worried about attacks on Pearl Harbor that he had persuaded Admiral Stark to press the army for a joint plan of defense for immediate reaction against surprise attack. But when Nomura came to Washington, and on March 12 had his first meeting with Admiral Turner, that admiral switched gears. Nomura gave his assurance that Japan would not undertake any further aggressive moves in Asia, because that is what Nomura had been told in Tokyo. Turner was convinced. A few weeks later Turner had a report from the army that claimed that Oahu was the "strongest fortress in the world" and the only danger might come from sabotage by persons of Japanese ancestry. If the Japanese were so foolish as to send an attack force against Hawaii, the army report said, it would come under attack at a distance of 750 miles from army and navy aircraft and could not possibly succeed.

No one thought to count the number of aircraft that were to undertake this glorious defense of the islands, and no one asked Admiral Kimmel when General Marshall at about that time assured President Roosevelt that the army air defenses made Hawaii impregnable to attack.

Kimmel tried to get information from Washington and asked Admiral Stark to be sure he was kept informed of the information received by code breaking. Stark replied that he had instructed the Office of Naval Intelligence to keep Pearl Harbor adequately informed.

ONI did not.

Kimmel's intelligence officer, Commander Edwin T. Layton, made a personal attempt through an old acquaintance, the head of the Far East section of Naval Intelligence. He was brushed off with the note that Washington would not send any intercepted messages because it was Washington's job to evaluate intelligence, and that the fleet should not worry until the time for action arrived. In other words, the Pacific Fleet was to wait for an actual attack, which would come as a surprise, because Washington refused to do its job and also refused to let the fleet do its job properly.

The navy department in Washington was alive with feuding officers working against one another. The center of the storm was Admiral Turner, whose aspirations to become chief of naval operations were well known and encouraged by Admiral Stark. Turner took many responsibilities on himself. In his own mind, the key to his importance lay in his ability to control information and to distribute it upward but not downward, which would do him no good. And he feuded constantly with the Office of Naval Intelligence. In May 1941, the head of ONI had noted on an intelligence summary that he thought the Japanese would move very soon. Turner had seen the note and scribbled on it: "I don't think the Japs are going to jump, now or ever."

This was the man who ultimately controlled Pearl Harbor's access to intelligence materials, and his prejudices meant that the people at Pearl Harbor weren't getting the raw material for independent evaluation of the enemy intentions.

By May 1941, Admiral Kimmel was growing worried about his ability to defend anything. Admiral Stark had plans to transfer three battleships, four cruisers, and a carrier and two squadrons of destroyers to the Atlantic. Again Kimmel protested and again he won with the President, but he did not secure his other request, for more information from Washington about Japanese movements.

On July 25, the Japanese marched into Southern Indochina. The next day the State Department announced the freezing of all Japanese funds in the United States and a trade embargo on oil. This had not been President Roosevelt's intention. He had told Secretary of Interior Harold L. Ickes that he had wanted to "slip the noose around Japan's neck and give it a jerk now and then," but the hawks in the Department of State went much further and declared the embargo on the same day that General MacArthur, America's most famous soldier, was ordered back to active duty with the American Army as chief of U.S. forces in the Far East. The implication to Japan was obvious; the Americans were preparing for war, and it played directly into the hands of the hawks in the Japanese Imperial Army who were itching for the war to begin.

Given very little information from a Washington naval establishment that was certain no attack would be launched against Pearl Harbor, the

Pacific Fleet command struggled valiantly to put together the shreds of intelligence it could get, much of it from partial intercepts of the Japanese radio-coded traffic picked up by Commander Joseph Rochefort's radio intelligence unit at Pearl Harbor. The Japanese had recently changed their codes, and the code breakers were just learning to read the new code so the information was slight and imperfect, but it gave some clues. For example, in the first week of November they were able to deduce that the Japanese fleet was preparing for some sort of major action, from the nature and extent of the radio traffic, a fact not given them by Washington.

But a little information can be a dangerous thing: In mid-November, when there were no transmissions from the aircraft carriers, the Pacific Fleet command deduced that they were laid up in port replenishing. They could not have been further wrong! The carriers were on their way to the Kuril Islands, and from now on carrier radio silence would be maintained until the Pearl Harbor attack!

In that month of November, the radio traffic intercepted at Pearl Harbor indicated that operations were being made in Tokyo for a southern advance through the South China Sea under cover of airfields in Indochina. The probable objectives would be Malaya, the Dutch East Indies, and the Philippines.

By November 24, Pearl Harbor was expecting a Japanese move in the Far East. Washington was suddenly, belatedly, aware of danger, and both the army and the navy high command were urging President Roosevelt to do something to keep the talks with Japan going — they were about to collapse with no progress — until more bombers could be flown to the Philippines and more defenses added to Wake Island and Guam. No one, Admiral Stark told Admiral Kimmel in a letter that week, would be surprised at a Japanese surprise attack.

But, of course, he did not mean on Hawaii.

Instead of responding softly, to give the army and navy a little more time for preparations that were suddenly beginning, the State Department chose this moment — November 26, 1941 — for Secretary Cordell Hull to make what a veteran Japanese diplomat called "a declaration of war." Hull delivered to the Japanese ambassador an uncompromising list of ten absolute preconditions that had to be met by Japan before the United States would even consider resuming trade or lifting its oil embargo. The Japanese could not accept the ten conditions. There was no place else to go, no room for compromise with the ultimatum. Ambassador Nomura, and the man who had been sent out from Tokyo by the Foreign Office to help him, Ambassador Kurusu, left the Department of State building that day shaking with anger and frustration.

Now Washington was aware of the possibility of an attack, but not on Hawaii. The army ordered the transfer of half the P-40 fighter planes of the army air force to Wake and Midway Islands and said it was sending a new contingent of B-17s to the Philippines. Obviously no attack was expected on Pearl Harbor, so Admiral William F. Halsey made ready to set out with a load of aircraft for Wake, half expecting to meet the Japanese fleet somewhere in the vicinity of the atoll. On the afternoon of November 27, Washington finally issued a war warning, noting that the negotiations with the Japanese had broken off. But the warning was for war in the Philippines or Malaya.

On Friday, November 28, the carrier *Enterprise* left Pearl Harbor with its task force of cruisers and destroyers. Halsey was on his way looking for trouble. He did not take any battleships along — they would just slow him down — so he left the battleships of the task force in the shelter of Pearl Harbor where the water was so shallow no one ever expected the Japanese to try a torpedo attack.

For the next week all the American carrier task forces at sea sent out air searches, and the southern and western approaches to Hawaii were carefully scouted morning and evening by PBY-5 patrol bombers. A unit of PBYs was sent from Midway to Wake to conduct searches all along that route. In the week before December 7, U.S. Navy air searches scoured 2 million square miles of the Pacific without spotting a single Japanese ship. But they did not search the northern waters; the conventional wisdom held that an attack would come from the other side, and there were

131

not enough aircraft to search all around. The army had only its 6 B-17s. The navy had only 81 long-range PBYs. To maintain comprehensive daily surveillance around the compass would have required 250 PBYs, each searching an 8-degree wedge of ocean out as far as 700 miles. If any enemy appeared within their purview they could find the ships a full day before they could attack. But with the planes available they could search only 40 percent of the compass, leaving 60 percent open to attack.

Admiral Kimmel did not have the aircraft or the people to fly them to cover all the search areas. Some decisions had to be made. One was to leave the area due north unsearched, because there was nothing up there but boundless sea for thousands of miles, sea and bad weather that should discourage any sensible navigator. And this was precisely why the Japanese had chosen the northern route, over the violent objections of Admiral Nagumo, who wanted to take the conventional road from the Marshalls, coming from the south. So in addition to all the difficulties in conflicts of command and lack of information, one had to add the factor of a bad guess.

All that week before December 7, the Americans were searching the air for the Japanese who might possibly (no one in command really believed) be coming to attack Pearl Harbor. But they were searching in the wrong places.

All during that last week of peace, the first week of December, Commander Layton worked on a comprehensive report for Admiral Kimmel, trying to place all the major elements of the Japanese fleet from intelligence reports, as the aircraft searched in the southwest and northwest approaches to Pearl Harbor. The big question was Where were the Japanese aircraft carriers? No amount of deduction or fragments of radio intercept helped place them. All the Japanese carriers had vanished from radio contact after they returned from fleet exercises after the first week of November. Finally some of the carriers were identified as going to join that body of the Japanese fleet moving into southern waters and actually preparing to attack Malaya. But the carriers of Carrier Division One and Carrier Division Two were unaccounted for and were presumed to be in port, loading supplies and replenishing their aircraft. One of the intelligence analysts at Pearl Harbor, Lieutenant John A. Williams, had a gut feeling that the carriers were at sea and up to something that boded no good for the American Navy, but hunches did not make for naval decisions, and he had absolutely nothing with which to back his belief.

On December 1, the command at Pearl Harbor was sure that something was up, some Japanese assault was planned, on the other side of the Pacific Ocean.

That day in Washington the navy cryptographers deciphered a Japanese message from Tokyo that included a copy of a message from Tokyo to the Japanese ambassador in Berlin assuring the Germans that war was about to break out between Japan and the Western powers. Another part of the message told Admiral Nomura and Ambassador Kurusu "to prevent the United States from becoming unduly suspicious." To an intelligence officer, this statement should have been a red flag warning of impending operations against America. The Japanese diplomats were being told to play for time until something happened.

Had Admiral Kimmel been sent this message he might have known what was going to happen, beyond his worst nightmares. But he was not included on the distribution list.

Still, ONI in Washington had the wind up, and Captain McCollum, head of the Far East branch, took his findings to Admiral Stark's office before a bevy of admirals, including Admiral Turner. He asked Stark if both the Asiatic and Pacific fleets had been alerted to the danger of war. Stark said yes, they had, but it was not true.

On December 2 there was still no information about the aircraft carriers, and this worried Admiral Kimmel. He asked intelligence officer Layton if the Japanese carriers might not at that moment be rounding Diamond Head and was told that they might well be for all Layton knew.

On December 3, there was still no information about the Japanese carriers. They did learn at Pearl Harbor that day that the Japanese had ordered the destruction of the "Purple machines" in London, Hong Kong, Singapore, and Manila. But they did not know what a Purple machine was, because Washington had never let them in on the secrets of decrypting the Japanese messages. Commander Layton asked the fleet security officer, who had recently come from Washington, and learned that Purple was a Japanese electronic coding machine. The destruction of these machines must mean that the Japanese were prepared for anything.

December 4. Pacific Fleet headquarters learned that the Japanese consulate was burning its codes and records. In Washington Admiral Turner continued to withhold information from the Pacific Fleet.

December 5. That day an unidentified submarine was reported off Hawaii, and two suspicious underwater contacts were made south of Diamond Head. That afternoon the destroyer *Selfridge* made sonar contact with a suspicious object but did not drop any depth charges because it might be a Japanese submarine and "the United States was not at war with Japan." Ship captains had long since been warned not to take any precipitate action that might ignite conflict.

But that day Lieutenant William W. Outerbridge, USN, took command of the destroyer *Ward*, a ship that except for the captain was manned entirely by a crew of naval reservists from St. Paul, Minnesota, young men all fired up to go to war and win it for Uncle Sam.

Lieutenant Outerbridge then accompanied his

destroyer division commander, Commander E. G. Fullenwider, in a call on Captain Morrison, the Inshore Patrol Commander at Pearl Harbor. There they talked about the duties of the Inshore Patrol, which was part of the Fourteenth Naval District. Some changes had been made, said Captain Morrison, showing them a dispatch from the Fourteenth Naval District:

"Any submarine not escorted and not operating in the restricted area, or rather the area restricted for use of submarines, is to be attacked immediately and sunk."

Fullenwider and Outerbridge laughed over the dispatch. Of course no one had seen an unauthorized submarine around those parts for years. Besides, they said, they knew they would have plenty of warning before any attacks would develop.

But Outerbridge left the meeting understanding that he was going on sentry duty, and that he must always be prepared to warn the Fourteenth Naval District of any thing unusual.

That day Captain McCollum tried to send a war warning to Pearl Harbor but was stopped by Admiral Turner, who said that his messages of late November had given plenty of warning. So McCollum's message was never sent.

December 6, 1941. All the information at Pearl Harbor indicated war was coming immediately, but war in the South China Sea, not war at Pearl Harbor. The thought that Pearl Harbor might be the focus of attack was far from all minds, except that of Admiral Kimmel, who wanted to send the battleships to sea for safety. He was talked out of it by his chief of staff and his operations officer, who said that without the carriers the battleships would be too vulnerable. They had many other objections: it would interrupt the training routine, it would waste fuel, and it would raise an alarm that might be totally unnecessary. Kimmel allowed himself to be persuaded to leave the battleships in harbor.

Captain Laurance Safford of ONI saw that war was imminent and drafted a message to Wake Island in particular, telling them to destroy their codebooks. He took the message to the assistant director of naval communications, who refused to send it without the approval of his superior, Admiral Leigh Noyes. A meeting was held in the office of the deputy chief of naval operations. Admiral Noyes said the message impinged on Admiral Turner's authority, predicting war immediately. Safford said it was a matter of hours. Noyes, who had been persuaded by Admiral Turner, said the Japanese were bluffing. So Noyes would not send the dispatch. No warning was sent to Wake Island. A toned-down version of the message was sent to Pearl Harbor, where it impressed nobody. And that was the last official action of the day, December 6, in Washington. Pearl Harbor, too, closed down that evening with no sense that anything unusual was about to happen in the Western Hemisphere.

Chapter 9

Attack!

On the morning of December 6, 1941, Lieutenant Outerbridge took the destroyer *Ward* to sea for his first cruise. They would be out for three days, and then would come back into port for one day, and then go out for three more days.

Lieutenant Outerbridge instructed his executive officer: They were to be prepared to open fire, they were to be prepared to use depth charges, they were to deal with any eventuality within the capabilities of their ship.

It was a beautiful day to be sailing out of Pearl Harbor, the breeze was light and warm, and when they got to sea, it was a question of drifting across the buoys and listening for propeller noises, easy duty it seemed.

Lieutenant Outerbridge was very favorably impressed with his crew, the young men full of zeal and enthusiasm. The officers all seemed to know their jobs and did them competently and with grace. He gave silent thanks to his predecessor for the training of the crew.

The *Ward*'s job in the Inshore Patrol was to watch over a square 3 miles to each side, just off the entrance to Pearl Harbor, and the harbor entrance itself. Their major instrument for submarine search was the sonic detector.

That night of December 6, the army air force headquarters on Hawaii had word that the B-17 flight that was on its way to shore up the Philippine defense force would arrive at Hawaii en route the next morning. In such cases it was the air force habit to ask Radio Station KGMB to stay on the air all night long, so the pilots of the bombers could home in on the radio signal. This night was no exception, and KGMB was asked to broadcast all night and complied as it always had, for it was being paid to do so by the army air force. So those who stayed up late in this Christmas season, and the Japanese at sea, had the pleasant sounds of big band music to lull them that night.

As Americans of the fleet were sleeping, early on the morning of December 7, 1941, the Japanese of the submarine force that had approached Oahu in the last few days were moving into action.

The I-boats carrying the midget submarines were all in position, and long before dawn they began launching the small craft, whose task was to penetrate the harbor and attack. As noted, Ensign Sakamaki, whose gyrocompass did not work, elected to attack anyhow, and he and his crewman got into the midget submarine and it was released from the *I-24*. They began to steer the midget submarine toward what they thought was the entrance to Pearl Harbor.

At about two o'clock on the morning of December 7, two converted minesweepers entered the channel on their routine duty of sweeping the channel early in the morning with their gear. At 3:58 the watch aboard the *Ward* had a flashing light signal from the minesweeper *Condor*.

"We have sighted a suspicious object, which looks like a submarine. It appears to be standing to the westward from our present position."

The signalman aboard the *Ward* acknowledged the signal and Skipper Outerbridge was notified. He ordered General Quarters. The ship got up speed to 20 knots and closed the *Condor*, asking for additional information. The ships exchanged several messages over voice radio. After reaching the position of the *Condor* the *Ward* turned west, toward Barber's Point, and searched. The search revealed nothing. After half an hour or so, Lieutenant Outerbridge decided that if it had been a submarine, it had evaded them. He told the watch to secure the ship from General Quarters, and told the executive officer, who was on duty, to let the men sleep in the next morning since they had been up so late this night. Then Skipper Outerbridge went back to bed in his sea cabin.

At four o'clock the watch changed. Lieutenant H. T. Doughty, the executive officer, went off watch and Lieutenant O. W. Goepner, another reserve officer, took over as officer of the deck. Not long after going on duty, he awakened the captain to report that the repair ship *Antares* was approaching the harbor with a steel barge in tow. The captain acknowledged sleepily, and went back to sleep.

Coming down from the north Pacific, the Japanese of the carrier striking force were up at four o'clock in the morning and getting ready for their attack, with a breakfast of snapper and rice. The Japanese force was about 325 miles north of Oahu. In the radio room the operators were still listening to the lilting music of Honolulu radio station KGMB, whose uninterrupted broadcast showed that the Americans suspected nothing.

The aircrews assembled in their ready rooms for the final briefing, and then the pilots got ready to man their planes. Just before six o'clock the carriers turned into the wind and the launching of the planes began. Commander Fuchida, the leader of the air strike, was given a headband by the crew of *Akagi*, and he tied it around his helmet before he slipped into the cockpit of his plane.

The Zero fighters took off first. One fighter pilot miscalculated and crashed into the sea on takeoff, but the pilot was picked up by a destroyer. Another Zero began to cough, and the pilot had to pull out of the formation and wait for permission to land and abort for engine trouble. But those were the only losses. As soon as the attacking fighters were launched, so was the combat air patrol that would protect the carrier fleet from any surprises from the Americans.

Next the high-level bombers went off, with Commander Fuchida's plane going first. Each bomber carried a pilot, a bombardier observer, and a radio operator. Each crewman had a pistol, a map of Oahu, and survival gear in case he had to land in the sea.

After the level bombers got off the decks of the six carriers, the torpedo bombers began to take off, each with its own three-man crew, too. Then the dive-bombers began to launch, and soon there were 185 planes in the air, the first wave of the attack against Pearl Harbor: forty-three fighters, forty-nine high-level bombers, forty torpedo planes, and fifty-one dive-bombers.

For fifteen minutes the aircraft circled the ship formation and formed up into their flight pattern, checking to be sure there would be no more aborts. At 6:20 Commander Fuchida led his level bombers across the bow of the *Akagi*, and everyone knew that that was the signal. The other planes formed up and followed, and the attack unit moved off in the direction of Oahu.

As soon as the last plane left the decks of the carriers, Admiral Nagumo ordered the fleet to turn south at 20 knots, to be closer to Oahu when the time came to recover the aircraft. On the hangar decks of the carriers, the plane handlers worked furiously to prepare the second strike.

The pilots and aircrews assembled in the ready rooms and prepared to go. Commander Genda, the genius who had planned the whole attack, gave some last-minute instructions. He told Lieutenant Chihaya, the commander of the *Akagi*'s second dive-bomber echelon, to check on the enemy antiaircraft fire. Genda was thinking about a third strike that day, and if the antiaircraft fire was too strong, he would not employ any torpedo planes on the third strike.

At 6:30 that morning the air attack force was still an hour and a half away from Hawaii. The captain of the *Antares* was preparing to enter Pearl Harbor when he saw what he thought was the conning tower of a small submarine. At the same time the object was seen by the helmsman of the destroyer USS *Ward*.

Lieutenant Outerbridge was still snoring in his sea cabin when he was rudely awakened by Lieutenant Goepner. Once was enough, Skipper Outerbridge thought, for a really inconsequential matter like the report on the *Antares*. Twice was too much.

"Captain, come onto the bridge," said Lieutenant Goepner.

"Now look here, Goepner," the skipper protested. "That's stern talk for the Officer of the Deck to be giving. You know it means I have got to come to the bridge. I've only been here one day, but I want you to realize that giving commands like that is serious business. I fully expect to find something up there."

"Captain, come to the bridge" was the imperious answer. So Lieutenant Outerbridge got up to the bridge on the double, sensing that something was not right.

Goepner pointed. "We've been watching that object. It appears to be following the *Antares*. It looks like a buoy, but it's moving and we think it is a submarine."

Outerbridge took a hard look.

"I believe that's a submarine," he said. "Go to General Quarters."

Goepner sounded the gong and the crew came to General Quarters at 6:35.

"If that is a submarine," said Outerbridge, "we will attack."

"I'll go to my battle station," said Goepner. He was the gunnery officer.

"Yes, Doughty will take the deck."

Lieutenant Goepner ordered the guns all loaded. The depth charges were all set for "ready." The destroyer was an old four-stack World War I model, and she had only two boilers fired up and could only make about 20 knots. So at 20 knots they went after the submarine.

As they approached, Captain Outerbridge wondered whether he should shoot or ram.

But since he did not know how big the submarine was, he decided not to ram, because they had the speed up to 24 knots and the ramming might knock the bottom out of the destroyer.

So he decided to shoot and drop depth charges.

At about 75 yards off he ordered the gunners to open fire. Gun No. 1 fired first, and missed. Gun No. 3 fired next, and the shell hit the submarine at the base of the conning tower, there was a feather of water, and the shell appeared to penetrate. Some of the men said they saw a hole in the submarine. They passed by the submarine so close that other men said they thought the destroyer was going to ram. They dropped four depth charges, the charges exploded, and the submarine sank.

After the submarine sank they looked around and saw a white sampan that was in the restricted area where it had no right to be. They decided to investigate it. But on the way, they sent a message to Pearl Harbor saying that they had attacked a submarine, and a second message saying that they had attacked with guns, which meant a surfaced submarine.

The *Ward* then chased the sampan, which hove to. They went alongside and the sampan captain, a Japanese, came out of the cabin waving a white flag, which they thought was odd. They sent for the Coast Guard, which sent a cutter from Honolulu Harbor, which then escorted the sampan into Honolulu Harbor.

At about the same time Fourteenth Naval District also had a report from Patrol Wing 2 that a patrol plane had depth bombed and sunk a small submarine off the entrance to Pearl Harbor. So two of the Japanese miniature submarines were accounted for, but no one had yet really sounded an alert at Pearl Harbor!

Shortly after 7:00 A.M. the Japanese carriers turned east into the wind again, and increased speed to 24 knots. The second strike began to launch. The sky was quite cloudy, with visibility of 12 miles and ceiling around 5,000 feet. The 36 fighters took off first — no aborts this time. In this second wave came 54 horizontal bombers, which would strike the American airfields, Hickam, Kaneohe Naval Air Station, and Ford Island. The 78 dive-bombers in this wave would strike the ships in Pearl Harbor a second time. One dive-bomber did not make it, the engine ran rough and the flight was scratched. But all the other aircraft got off safely and began winging their way toward Oahu to follow on the heels of the first wave. A total of 350 Japanese planes were going in to attack.

Admiral Nagumo and Admiral Kusaka stood on the bridge of the *Akagi* and watched as the planes disappeared into the murk ahead. Commander Genda watched for a little while and then went to the control room to await the signal from Fuchida that the air attack was beginning.

In Washington that morning, General Marshall arrived at his office to learn that big events were brewing in Asia. The navy had the same information, from code breaks. That morning the Japanese message of ultimatum arrived. General

Marshall sent an alert message to Hawaii:

"Japanese are presenting at 1:00 P.M. Eastern Standard Time today what amounts to an ultimatum. Also they are under orders to destroy their code machine immediately. Just what significance the hour set may have we do not know, but be on the alert, accordingly. Inform naval authorities of this communication. Marshall."

There were problems, atmospheric and other, with army communications that day, so the army sent the message by Western Union, the commercial telegraph and cable company. The message did not have a priority designation. When it reached Hawaii, it was pigeonholed for routine delivery to Fort Shafter. It sat as the minutes ticked away.

At sea, about 250 miles west of Hawaii, Admiral Halsey's Task Force 8, built around the carrier *Enterprise*, was heading back to Pearl Harbor after delivering its load of aircraft to Wake Island. The admiral was still expecting trouble, so he sent off a search patrol that dawn to look for Japanese carriers. On the hangar and flight deck, the dive-bomber squadron was getting ready to fly off and make the trip to Hawaii as the carrier steamed home.

On the northern tip of Oahu the two soldiers manning the Opana Mobile Radar station had been there since they went on duty at 4:00 A.M. Private Joseph L. Lockard was senior, and the junior member of the team was Private George E. Elliott. At 7:00 A.M. they were scheduled to shut down operations and go off duty. They got ready to leave when suddenly Lockard saw a mess of dots on their screen, so many that it was hard to think of them as blips. He watched for a couple of minutes and counted more than fifty images, at first 132 miles from Oahu. Elliott suggested that they telephone the combat information center, but Lockard said it might be an aberration of the machine. But Elliott persisted, so Lockard agreed to telephone, on the basis that it would be good exercise for the information center to deal with an unexpected report. The call was made and consumed about five minutes, during which time the blips moved 25 miles nearer to Oahu.

Theoretically the information center was manned by a group of plotters who moved markers around a big table, symbolizing the movement of aircraft. Above them at the second-floor level was a large balcony where the controller and pursuit officer sat and watched. It was their job to order planes up to intercept enemy planes or supposed enemy planes, but this morning nothing was expected except one flight of B-17s en route to the Philippines. The controller had left early and so had all the plotters. The switchboard operator, Private Joseph Mc-Donald, thought he was the only one on duty, but as he took this call from Elliott at the radar station he saw Lieutenant Kermit Tyler, a brand-new pursuit officer who had served only one day previously on the job.

When Private Elliott said what he thought the radarmen were seeing, Private McDonald was impressed enough to ask Lieutenant Tyler to pick up the phone. Private Lockard got on the other end and told what they had seen — the biggest sighting he had ever seen — and gave the course and speed. Tyler was impressed. It might be a big group of planes from one of the carriers. Then he remembered that KGMB had been on the air all night and that he had heard that when B-17s were coming in the radio station stayed on all night, so he attributed the number of blips to the B-17s that were supposed to be coming in. Lockard did not tell him that he had seen more than fifty blips. That news might have alerted Lieutenant Tyler that there were too many blips. The coming of the B-17s was a matter of security not to be shared with privates like Lockard, so not knowing how many blips there were, Lieutenant Tyler said not to worry about the sighting and hung up the phone.

At this time, when the radarmen were watching the Japanese attack coming in without knowing what they were seeing, the destroyer *Ward* had established another submarine contact out by the entrance to Pearl Harbor. She dropped more depth charges and saw a black oil bubble about 300 yards astern. Skipper Outerbridge believed he had gotten to another submarine.

On the northern tip of Oahu, the radarmen

stayed on duty, fascinated with the sight of these blips coming in so steadily. From 7:20 to 7:39, when they lost the blips due to radar distortion by the mountains, they tracked the incoming flight.

Four minutes before contact was lost, the reconnaissance plane from the cruiser *Chikuma*, which was lazily circling over Pearl Harbor, radioed back to the Japanese fleet:

"Enemy formation at anchor; nine battleships, one heavy cruiser, six light cruisers are in the harbor." Then came a meteorological report: "Wind direction from eighty degrees, speed fourteen meters, clearance over enemy feet one thousand seven hundred meters, cloud density seven." Then the *Chikuma* plane headed back to the fleet, its job done.

In Hawaii the army was not talking to the navy and the navy was not talking to the army. The navy submarine alert was not communicated to army headquarters, where it might at least have triggered enough response to force the army air force to move its aircraft from their wingtip-to-wingtip positions on the fields.

Nor did the navy learn anything about the "more than fifty blips" coming in from the north, which would at least have told them where the Japanese carriers were located. Each service was serene in its ignorance of what was happening and not at all concerned about the moments ahead. At Fourteenth Naval District headquarters, Admiral Claude C. Bloch was inclined to believe that the sighting by the *Ward* were just the result of too much enthusiasm.

So when the Pacific Fleet duty officer telephoned Admiral Kimmel he had no knowledge that in Washington the secretaries of State, War, and Navy were waiting anxiously for a statement expected momentarily from the Japanese that they thought would presage war, that General Marshall had sent a war warning that was still resting in a cubbyhole in the telegraph office, or that the radarmen at Opana Point on North Oahu were watching a whole armada of blips closing on Oahu. The duty officer reported the activities of the *Ward*. Standing alone, they seemed odd but no cause for alarm. Had they been added to all the other factors, all separated and unknown to the command, they would have raised the hackles on the back of Admiral Kimmel's neck. Just now he was wondering how long it would take him to dispose of this problem so that he could get down to the serious business of his regular Sunday morning golf game with General Short.

Chapter 10

The First Wave

In spite of all the failures and coincidences of the moment — the failure of Washington to keep Pearl Harbor notified of developments and dangers, and the coincidence of the arrival of the B-17s expected from California on almost the same course the Japanese attack unit followed into Oahu — there was still plenty of reason for Pearl Harbor not to have been surprised by the Japanese attack until the moment it came.

The Japanese submarine force that had invaded the Hawaiian waters numbered twenty-seven I-boats, 2,000-ton submarines, eleven of which carried small aircraft and five of which carried midget submarines. On December 5 they had been in position ringing Oahu. The first American naval contact with the Japanese submarine force had been made early on the morning of December 7, four hours before the air attack, when the converted minesweeper *Condor* sighted the periscope of a midget submarine less than 2 miles from the harbor buoy at Pearl Harbor.

The *Condor* had passed the word of the sighting to the *Ward* by blinker and then gone about her own business. The *Ward* had then begun seriously to hunt for submarines; her findings have been reported. But there were other sightings. At 6:30 A.M. a navy Catalina flying boat spotted that same little submarine in about the same place and dropped smoke pots to mark the spot. That is when the *Ward* swung into action and sank that particular midget submarine. But the *Ward*'s message about this contact was the first sent out; neither the *Condor* nor the navy search plane made any report of its sightings, so the Fourteenth Naval District and the Pearl Harbor command were kept in the dark by their own people, in a very serious failure of communications.

Even when the *Ward* report came in it was delayed because it had been sent by coded message and the yeoman who received it was, as naval historian Samuel Eliot Morison remarked, "not very bright" so he did not see any urgency in the message. Thus the duty officer of Fourteenth Naval District did not get the message until well after seven o'clock.

The harbor control at Pearl Harbor that day malfunctioned completely. The gate in the antitorpedo net was opened at 4:45 in the morning to let through the *Antares*, which was towing a barge, and another minesweeper as well. The gate was allowed to remain open until 8:40, during which time at least one of the Japanese midget submarines sneaked into Pearl Harbor. Another of the little submarines ran onto a reef east of the entrance channel and sat there for many minutes, unobserved by anyone. Ensign Sakamaki followed instinct, since his compass was not working, and instinct and the currents led him on a long chase around the westward side of the island toward the north shore. He was not observed either, as he tried to fight the currents to enter Pearl Harbor. Admiral Kimmel remained blissfully unaware of anything at all until nearly 7:30. By that time, Commander Fuchida's force was just about to break through the cloud cover and sight the island of Oahu, to begin the run in for the attack.

On that sunny morning of December 7, 1941, the weather and fleet reports from the observation plane of the Japanese cruiser *Chikuma* were relayed by the Japanese flagship to Commander Fuchida's Pearl Harbor assault force.

When the green shores and gray-purple mountains of Oahu came into view Commander Fuchida picked up his signal gun and fired a flare, the announcement that they had arrived in attack range and were to deploy as planned. If they had achieved surprise Fuchida would fire one flare. If they had not, then he would fire two flares. If the surprise was complete, then the torpedo bombers would attack first. If not, then the dive-bombers would go first.

At 7:40 Commander Fuchida knew they had

achieved complete surprise, a knowledge confirmed by the *Chikuma* plane report. He fired a single flare.

The attack could begin.

But then Fuchida noticed that the fighters were not responding as they should. One group did not take the proper formation. After waiting about ten seconds, Fuchida then repeated the signal. But Lt. Commander Kakuichi Takahashi misread this second flare as the second of two, and he swooped down immediately with his dive-bombers for the run on battleship row, Ford Island and Hickam Field. So by error the dive-bombers struck first. Fuchida was upset, but soon enough he saw that the surprise was so complete it did not matter who attacked first. The Americans were completely unprepared.

The *Chikuma* pilot had reported nine battleships in the harbor, Fuchida saw seven, but there were actually eight. Commander Fuchida did not see the battleship *Pennsylvania*, which was in dry dock, and the *Chikuma* pilot had mistakenly counted the old battleship *Utah*, which was now used as a target ship, as a contemporary warship. At 7:49 Commander Fuchida gave the signal to attack.

At the Japanese anchorage of the Combined Fleet, in Hashirajima, Admiral Yamamoto was playing shogi with Chief of Staff Ugaki when a messenger came from the radio room to announce that the signal had come, the attack was on and it had achieved complete surprise. Admiral Ugaki excused himself to go to the operations room and await developments, but Yamamoto was completely calm.

The first attack was made on the north shore, at the Naval Air Station of Kaneohe, where a group of fighters and dive-bombers moved in as soon as Commander Fuchida signaled the attacks. Before 7:50 the first plane strafed the air station and the ramps and planes moored in the water. Then the dive-bombers followed, and the air was filled with bombing, strafing planes. Patrol Wing 1, stationed at Kaneohe, had only thirty-six PBYs at the moment and a few miscellaneous aircraft. Four were moored in the bay, about a thousand yards apart. The rest were parked on the ramp close together, except for four in the hangar.

The first bomb hit squarely on Kaneohe station's only fire truck. Then the planes began to go up. The planes on the water began to catch fire and burn.

The officer of the day called Bellows Field to warn them of the attack and was told that he must be joking. Someone else telephoned Hickam Field, and was not believed that there was an air attack going on.

Other Japanese planes hit Ewa Field before there was any attack on Pearl Harbor; twenty-one Zero fighters came in over the Waianae Mountains and strafed the parked aircraft, destroying half of them. They destroyed or damaged nine of the eleven Wildcat fighter planes, eighteen of the thirty-two scout bombers, and six of eight utility planes.

One group of torpedo bombers split into two eight-plane sections and headed for the west side of Pearl Harbor. The other group split into two groups of twelve planes each and headed for battleship row.

Lt. Commander Itaya led his Zero fighters in, and remembered clearly what he saw:

"Pearl Harbor was still asleep in the morning mist. It was calm and serene inside the harbor, not even a trace of smoke from the ships at Oahu. The orderly groups of barracks, the wriggling white line of the automobile road climbing up to the mountaintop; fine objectives of attack in all directions. In line with these, inside the harbor, were important ships of the Pacific Fleet, strung out and anchored two ships side by side in an orderly manner."

Aboard those ships the men of the Pacific Fleet were following their Sunday-morning routine. As always in this period when watchfulness had been ordained for months, the fleet never completely relaxed, but in harbor on the weekends went to Condition 3 of readiness, which meant minimal manning. The morning watch, which would go off duty at 8:00 A.M., was tidying up after the night, wiping down the barrels of the guns and shining the brass. In the wardrooms, the officers who had the day watch were just finishing their breakfasts and the petty officers and the men were doing the same in their mess rooms. Of all the war ships in the harbor that morning, seventy fighting ships and twenty-four auxiliaries of various sorts, only one, the destroyer *Helm*, was underway. After the yeoman in the Fourteenth District radio room got his message from the *Ward* straight and decoded, he gave it to Lt. Commander Harold Kaminsky. But that had not been until 7:12, and Kaminsky had been on the telephone since, trying to raise people. Admiral Bloch had gotten through to the operations office, and the ready-duty destroyer *Monaghan* had been ordered to get underway, but she had not yet, and the standby destroyer was just getting up steam. There was action at Pearl Harbor by this time, but it was unseen.

From Honolulu came the sound of church bells, pealing for the congregation to come to the eight o'clock Mass for the Roman Catholics and eight o'clock Communion for the Protestants.

Lieutenant Graham D. Bonnell of the supply corps was aboard the USS *San Francisco*, which was undergoing an overhaul at the Pearl Harbor Navy Yard. Her engines had been torn down, there was no fuel aboard, the turrets were inoperative, and there was no ammunition aboard. That morning Lieutenant Bonnell was awake at around 7:30. He lay semiconscious for a few minutes, and then suddenly he was jerked awake by the sound of a screaming dive of an airplane. He looked out the porthole in the direction of Ford Island and saw a plane diving on one of the hangars. He saw the red balls on the airplane, but it did not register at the moment.

"I lay back on the bunk and thought to myself: Navy dive-bombers are the best in the world."

At about that time he heard a loud explosion and jumped out of his bunk again in time to see the hangar on Ford Island go up in smoke.

By that time the general alarm aboard the ship was sounding. . . .

Lt. Commander Kaminski had tried unsuccessfully to reach many people that morning, including Commander Vincent Murphy, the assistant war plans officer, who was duty officer at CINCPAC headquarters that weekend. He finally did get through to Lt. Commander R. B. Black, the assistant duty officer. Black found Murphy at his quarters, dressing for the day. Commander Murphy instructed Black to be sure that Kaminski had called Admiral Bloch, commander of the Fourteenth Naval District. Kaminski's line was busy; he was trying to call other people. Black got back to Murphy, who said he would try Kaminski and did, again without result. By the time Murphy got to his office the phone was ringing, and this time it was Lt. Commander Logan Ramsey of Patrol Wing 2, who reported that one of his planes had just sunk a submarine 1 mile off the entrance to Pearl Harbor. He told Ramsey that he had the same sort of report from a destroyer. They agreed that there was something funny going on.

Ramsey had just hung up the telephone when it rang again. Kaminski. He reported on the *Ward* action, and then Murphy called Admiral Kimmel, who had been up for half an hour, getting ready for the golf game with General Short. He also reported on the sampan. Kimmel wondered how much credence to put on the reports. So did Admiral Bloch, when he got the report that morning.

Murphy called Kimmel back when he had the sampan report of the stopping. Murphy had just said those words when a yeoman rushed into his office.

"There's a message from the signal tower saying that the Japanese are attacking Pearl Harbor and this is no drill," he shouted.

Murphy passed the word to the admiral, who slammed down the telephone and rushed outside his house, buttoning his white uniform jacket as he went.

Aboard the *Ward*, Lieutenant Outerbridge was excited by a new submarine contact near the Pearl Harbor entrance, and they dropped more depth charges and reported again to Fourteenth Naval District. Executive Officer Doughty came to the bridge and asked if would be possible to secure from General Quarters, because the men had been on full alert for a long time. It was just a few minutes before eight o'clock.

They heard several explosions. Doughty said he thought they were coming from the beach.

"That's probably that superhighway that's being built between Pearl Harbor and Honolulu, they're probably blasting this morning," said Outerbridge.

"No. It's not. Look over there. There are some planes coming straight down. It looks like they are bombing the place."

Outerbridge took a good look at the naval base. "My gosh," he said. "They are!"

Lt. Commander Ramsey was standing in the Ford Island Command Center, watching the color guard prepare to hoist the flag for the day. It was 7:55. He heard the scream of an airplane over the station and turned to a junior officer. "Get that fellow's name," he said. "I want to report him for about sixteen violations of the course and safety regulations." They watched the plane come down.

"Did you get his number?" asked Ramsey.

"No, but I think it must have been a squadron commander. I saw a band of red on the plane."

"Check all the squadrons and find out who is in the air," Ramsey demanded.

"I think I saw something black fall out of that plane."

Then an explosion emphasized the statement, and Ramsey knew what was happening. It was a Japanese plane and a Japanese bomb.

Rear Admiral William Rhea Furlong, commander of the service vessels of battle force, was strolling on the quarterdeck of his flagship, the minelayer *Oglala*, awaiting the word from the mess man that his breakfast was ready. The *Oglala* was sitting in the usual berth of the battleship *Pennsylvania*, which was in dry dock, nestled up against the cruiser *Helena*.

Furlong absentmindedly watched the planes come down, thinking of other matters, until he saw a bomb fall. What a stupid mistake for some pilot to be making; even a practice bomb could hurt somebody if it hit. But then the bomb hit and exploded, which no practice bomb should do. He also saw the red meatballs on the wings of the plane as it turned in the air. "Japanese," he shouted. "Man your stations!"

Lieutenant Bonnell's battle station was in the communications room in the superstructure of the *San Francisco*. He dressed in a hurry and headed for his battle station. The gun crews were organized and sent to other ships to help fight, since the *San Francisco* was as helpless as a hulk. . . .

Aboard the *Oglala* Admiral Furlong's men hoisted the flag: All Ships in Harbor Sortie . . .

Lt. Commander Ramsey ran across the corridor from the command center at Ford Island to the radio room, and ordered all radiomen on duty to send out a message in plain English.

From the radio tower of the headquarters on

Ford Island a message was sent out over the air-waves, a message that shook Americans in Washington and Manila.

"Air raid. Pearl Harbor. This is no drill."

The destroyer *Helm* was just entering West Loch, and she headed for the channel entrance. Her antiaircraft guns were firing, and she brought down a plane. As she passed through the submarine gate, her crewmen spotted the Japanese submarine grounded on Tripod Reef and fired at the midget sub.

Aboard the battleship *West Virginia*, Ensign Roland S. Brooks saw what he thought was an internal explosion aboard the battleship *California*, and gave the order from the bridge:

"Away fire and rescue party." This command brought men swarming up topside from below decks of the battleship, although he soon saw that the fire and smoke came not from the *California* but from the burning aircraft hangar on Ford Island.

Up above Pearl Harbor in the cane and pineapple fields, the rows of parked fighters at Wheeler Field stood wingtip to wingtip, with guards protecting them from sabotage on the ground, but nothing protecting them from the dive-bombers and fighters that swept down and smashed them. On Ford Island, the hangars were burning, and the bombs were raining down. About half the carrier-type planes on Ford Island

and most of the hangars were gone or burning, and so were many patrol planes, the bombs sending pieces of PBY high in the air, to smash back into the concrete or splash in the water.

At Hickam Field Colonel William E. Farthing, the field commander, was in the tower talking with the adjutant of what was still called the Hawaiian Air Force. They were waiting for the arrival of the B-17 flight from California, which was supposed to come in very soon that morning. Suddenly a large group of aircraft appeared from the north, and dive-bombers peeled off and began bombing the aircraft and facilities at Hickam. A fighter screeched down the streets of the officer's quarters, its guns spitting.

Hangar No. 9 was the first to go, its roof shattered by a bombers. The repair hangar was blasted. The enlisted men's hall took a direct hit, killing many men. The chapel was hit.

A bomb released the prisoners from the guardhouse and another hit the firehouse and smashed the water mains.

The bombers then concentrated on the B-17 bombers, parked wingtip to wingtip, but the B-17s were tough and at the end of the attack four of them were still in flyable condition, although they had been repeatedly bombed and strafed in those first minutes. Half of Hickam's planes had been destroyed and the base facilities were hit very hard.

At Wheeler Field, where the dive-bombers had

already set many planes afire, the Zeroes came back to strafe after hitting Hickam, and did more damage. There was no return fire from anti-aircraft guns, and they saw no American planes rising to meet them. The surprise was complete and a little awesome to the Japanese fliers. If the American pilots or gunners had wanted to fight, they could not have, because at night all the machine gun belts had been taken out of the planes and put into the hangars for safekeeping.

Wheeler Field that day housed ninety-one fighter planes, fifty-two modern P-40s and thirty-nine older P-36s. Half the planes were destroyed, including thirty of the P-40s. At the marine airfield at Ewa, which had first been strafed by fighters earlier, the returning dive-bombers destroyed nine of the eleven Wildcat fighters, eighteen of the thirty-two scout bombers, and six of eight utility planes.

So there were no American planes in the air to challenge the first wave of torpedo bombers as they swooped down on the ships in Pearl Harbor.

Admiral Kimmel had dashed out of his house on Makalapa Drive and onto the lawn of his neighbor, Captain John B. Earle, chief of staff to Admiral Bloch. He stood there with Mrs. Earle watching the events down below at battleship row. First they saw the dive-bombers flying over Ford Island and Hickam, making figure-8 patterns as they bombed and then strafed. They could see the rising sun insignia on the planes' wings very clearly.

Lieutenant Shigeharu Murata was the first to drop. Here was the proof or failure of all the work that had been done over all the months to modify the Japanese aerial torpedoes to run in shallow water. Would they work? Murata dropped his torpedo, and saw it crash against a battleship.

"Atarimashita," shouted the observer. "It hit!"

Those words were transmitted back to the flagship, where they allayed the many fears of Admiral Nagumo that the torpedo attack would be a fiasco. Commander Genda smiled broadly. His efforts had been crowned with success.

The *West Virginia* was the first ship to be hit; she took two torpedoes in rapid succession. The torpedoes knocked out all power, light, and communications. She listed, the list was corrected by flooding, and then she sank until the port bilge hit bottom and did not capsize. She was showered by debris from hits on other ships. *West Virginia* lost 2 officers and 103 men killed.

The *Oklahoma* was moored at Berth F-5 outboard of the battleship *Maryland*. A torpedo bomber came down to 60 feet above the water and put a torpedo into her. The pilot noticed that he was lower than the crow's nest of the battleship, and he zoomed above the deck. Then two other torpedo bombers loosed their torpedoes at the *Oklahoma*. The ship began to list. Soon the ship's executive officer, Commander J. L. Kenworthy, ordered abandon ship, and told the men to climb over the starboard side, for fear the battleship would capsize in the next few minutes.

A torpedo swept under the repair ship *Vestal* and hit the *Arizona*, but the real damage was done seconds later by a bomber, which dropped a bomb on the *Arizona*. The bomb hit beside the second turret, penetrated the forecastle, exploded in a forward magazine before it could be flooded, and wrecked the whole front end of the ship. Flames shot 500 feet in the air. Rear Admiral Isaac C. Kidd and Captain Franklin van Valkenburgh were killed on the bridge. All this before 7:56, as Admiral Kimmel watched. Then a second bomb went down the stack, a third hit the boat deck, a fourth hit No. 4 turret, and four more hit in the superstructure. *Arizona* sank so fast that she did not capsize, and more than a thousand men were trapped below deck, either burned to death or drowned. The ship lost four-fifths of her ship's complement.

The battleship *Tennessee* was moored inboard of the *West Virginia*, and so she was protected from torpedoes by the other ship. But she took two bombs, one on the center of Gun Turret No. 2 and the other on Gun Turret No. 3. But most of the damage to this ship was caused by flaming debris from the *Arizona*, which was 75 feet astern of the *Tennessee*. Five men were killed or missing, and one officer and twenty men were wounded.

The battleship *Nevada* was moored astern of

the *Arizona*. She had no ship tied up next to her. Her antiaircraft guns opened fire quickly and accurately. Her guns shot down at least one of the torpedo bombers. Fifty-caliber machine guns shot down another. Because of the shooting she suffered only one torpedo hit and that was forward; the 45-foot-long hole flooded many compartments but left the power plant intact. She managed to get underway, and that is what she was doing at the time of the end of the first attack.

The *Maryland* and the *Oklahoma* were moored next forward of the *Nevada*, and as noted the *Oklahoma* was hit early in the battle by three torpedoes. As the men were abandoning ship over the starboard side, two more torpedoes hit. The men were struggling to escape when the ship began to capsize. She rolled over and her masts stuck in the mud of the bottom. She lay with the starboard side of her bottom above water and part of the keel clear. Twenty officers and three hundred ninety-five men were killed or missing, and two officers and thirty men were wounded.

The *Maryland* was lucky. She was protected from the torpedoes by the *Oklahoma*. Her gunners shot down one torpedo plane before the pilot could launch his torpedo. She took only two bombs.

The *California*, the flagship of the cruiser squadron of the fleet, was hit by two torpedoes below the armor belt. She began to list to port, counterflooding was tried, but salt water got into the fuel tanks and she lost light and power, although she did not capsize. She was in trouble by the end of the first attack.

The last group of torpedo planes came in on the far side of Ford Island where the seaplane tender *Tangier*, the target ship *Utah*, and the crusiers *Raleigh* and *Detroit* were moored. The *Tangier* was unhurt in this attack, the old battle *Utah* was torpedoed twice by planes that thought she was a working battleship, and she capsized as Japanese planes returned to strafe.

The *Raleigh* was torpedoed, and the *Detroit* was near-missed by a torpedo in this first attack.

On the opposite side of the main channel, against battleship row, the minelayer *Oglala* was moored outboard of the light cruiser *Helena*. A torpedo plane, having missed the battleships, flew over and dropped its fish, which passed beneath the *Oglala* and smashed into the *Helena*, flooding an engine room. The antiaircraft gunners gave such a good account of themselves that the dive-bombers veered away from the *Helena* and sought other targets. But the *Oglala* was also damaged by that torpedo blast, and as the captain was deciding to abandon ship because she was sinking, a bomb fell between the two ships and caused total loss of power on the *Oglala*.

In the dry dock the *Pennsylvania*, flagship of the Pacific Fleet, and two destroyers, the *Cassin* and *Downes*, were captives, but their antiaircraft guns could be manned and they fought back against the dive-bombers that tried to attack them.

Kimmel watched from the Earle lawn in fascinated silence as the bombers hit battleship row. His car came up manned by his usual driver, and he dived into it. As it roared off down the hill Captain Freeland Daubin, commander of Submarine Squadron Four, jumped onto the runningboard and caught a ride. They reached the headquarters building down the hill just as the *California* was torpedoed in this first attack.

Chapter 11

The Attack Continues

After Lieutenant Outerbridge realized that Pearl Harbor was under attack he doubled his vigilance. The *Ward* brought two more boilers into use and then had full power available as the ship steamed around the entrance to Pearl Harbor searching for more submarine contacts.

The *Monaghan*, the ready-duty destroyer, had been notified of the attacks around the entrance to the harbor a few minutes before the air attacks began, and she came out at 8:27. Steaming toward the harbor entrance, off Ford Island, she noticed that the tender *Curtiss* was flying a flag indicating the presence of an enemy submarine. The lookouts checked and saw a midget submarine in the harbor, under fire from the ships *Medusa* and *Curtiss*. The submarine launched a torpedo at the *Curtiss*, which missed and hit a dock at Pearl City. The *Monaghan* then took the submarine under fire with her guns. The first shot was over the submarine, and hit a barge. The destroyer prepared to ram the submarine, which then fired another torpedo. The torpedo missed and exploded against the shore.

The *Monaghan* then rammed the midget submarine, passed over it as it sank, depth-charged it, and destroyed it. Her way from the ramming was so great that she collided with the barge that her first shot had hit, and had to back away. After firing a shot at a "submarine contact" that turned out to be a harbor buoy, the *Monaghan* then stood out into the channel and passed outside the harbor to join *Ward* in patrolling. Soon the *Helm* came out and then the destroyer *Aylwin*.

The destroyer *Helm*, meanwhile, was steaming in West Loch when her lookout spotted another Japanese midget submarine on Tripod Reef and fired at her. This was Ensign Sakamaki's submarine, and as the destroyer fired, the crewmen managed to get the midget sub off the reef and into the water. The *Helm* missed with her shots, and the midget began maneuvering again, but this time she got hopelessly lost and headed up around toward the north shore of the island, directly away from Pearl Harbor.

At 8:30, 1:30 EST, word of the attack ("This is not a drill") reached Washington just as the Japanese ambassadors were at the State Department to deliver their message breaking off the discussions that were supposed to have led to peace. Secretary Hull gave them short shrift, did not tell

172

them what they did not know — that the Japanese fleet had already attacked Pearl Harbor even as they were delivering their message — and sent them away brusquely. At first no one, including President Roosevelt, could believe that there had been an attack. Secretary of the Navy Frank Knox said he thought it must mean the Philippines but was assured that it was Pearl Harbor. Within a few minutes local radio stations all across America began to break into their quiet Sunday programs to announce that Pearl Harbor was even then under attack by Japanese aircraft.

In moments Secretary Knox was on the telephone to Admiral Bloch, receiving an eyewitness account of the aerial attack. Just then the stragglers from the first wave of Japanese attackers were heading back north and the second wave of the attack was coming in.

So, at that moment, were two flights of American aircraft — the B-17s from the West Coast and a group of planes from Admiral Halsey's carrier *Enterprise* that were coming in to land at Ford Island — on their way to Pearl Harbor.

The B-17s were very low on fuel and they headed for Hickam Field, to be told that the field was under attack and they could not land. The pilots then put down at airfields all over the island; one even landed on the navy golf course.

Eighteen Dauntless dive-bombers had taken off from the *Enterprise* early that morning and were coming in to what they thought was a landing at Ford Island. Instead they moved into a hail of fire from the second wave of attacking Japanese planes. One American dive-bomber was shot down by American antiaircraft guns, and four were lost to Zero fighters.

After the success of the first strike against the airfields the Japanese had complete control of the sky. After that first attack, not a single American navy plane rose into the air from Oahu to fight the Japanese. There was virtually nothing left to fly on the navy fields and at Hickam and Wheeler air bases. A handful of army fighters did get aloft from Bellows Field, a few miles south of Kaneohe, which had been hit in these first few minutes by one solitary strafer. The attack was so insignificant that a soldier crossing the barracks area on his way to church saw the Japanese plane and heard the firing and thought it was an American training plane practicing gunnery with blank cartridges. He did not even turn off his path to the church.

But that single strafer alerted Colonel Leonard D. Weddington, commander of the field. He called together ground crews, and they first dispersed the planes, then began to get them into action. The field had not been bothered by the Japanese because it was the home of a single observation squadron, and so they concentrated their efforts on the big fields. Since the field was not really damaged by the Japanese, they got their planes in the air and began attacking the Japanese. Luckily a squadron of P-40s had been attached to that field for a month of gunnery practice. The fighters took off — the only organized resistance on Oahu that morning. In all they claimed eleven enemy planes. But in fact they did not even slow the second wave of Japanese bombers as they came in to their designated targets.

By this time Admiral Kimmel had reached his office in the submarine base, and he stood at the window and watched the disaster that was continuing. A spent .50-caliber bullet broke through the glass and struck his jacket, raising a welt on his chest. It would have been better if it had killed him, the admiral said to his communications officer, who was standing next to him.

Outside, the second wave of Japanese dive-bombers that reached Pearl Harbor were concentrating on the battleship *Nevada*, which was underway and moving, although she was listing heavily. Tugs came out to help her and see that she did not block the channel. They managed to get the *Nevada* to Waipo Point, where she was beached.

In going after the *Nevada*, the Japanese bombers neglected the *Pennsylvania*, which, sitting in dry dock, was an easy target. One bomber did put a bomb into the *Pennsylvania*'s boat deck. Another bomber blew the bow off the destroyer *Shaw*, which was also in dry dock. The dry dock was flooded to prevent further damage from fire, but the fires were already creeping toward the magazines of the destroyers *Downes* and *Cassin*, which were also docked, and ten minutes after this strike, the two blew up. By nine o'clock that morning all of battleship row and all of Ford Island lay under a heavy curtain of smoke. The pilots of the Japanese planes could no longer see down through the murk, so they turned their attention to the northern side of Ford Island. The old battleship Utah got more attention and the three light cruisers nearby were all damaged.

Not long after Admiral Kimmel arrived at his headquarters the Pacific Fleet staff began to assemble. One of those to arrive by car from Honolulu, where he lived, was Commander Edwin Layton, the fleet intelligence officer. He checked in and was given first a list of the sunk and damaged ships, which appalled him so much he found it hard to concentrate. But he knew that his first task was to discover the whereabouts of the enemy fleet, because Admiral Kimmel would want to begin retaliating. Captain McMorris, the plans officer, called him into his plans office where several officers were sitting, stunned. Under cover of the racket from the two destroyers in the dry dock, which blew up, Commander Layton escaped to his own office, where he tried to find out the source of the Japanese planes that were surging over Pearl Harbor.

Layton had a call from the radio intelligence office, called Hypo. The duty officer told him they had gotten a direction finder bearing on the Japanese force. But the reading was bilateral. The Japanese were either due north or due south of Pearl Harbor, they could not tell which without another fix. Why could they not get a more accurate fix from the 75-foot antenna on a mountain north of Pearl Harbor? Layton wanted to know.

Because the telephone lines were down.

Why were the lines down?

Layton did not learn until later that it was because the army had pulled the plug on the phone lines when the attack began, without warning to the navy. Neither had the army ever relayed the bearings of that force spotted at Opana Point. So the navy got no information or help at all from the army.

Layton was down in the fleet operations room, laying out the opposite bearings, when Admiral Kimmel came in.

"Where is the enemy?" the admiral asked.

"Either due north of us or due south, sir," said Commander Layton.

"Well, dammit, which?"

"I can't tell you, sir. It could be either one."

The tension was relieved by a report that Japanese parachutists were landing on Oahu. One report placed the enemy troops at Barber's Point. But all that was found there was a lone mechanic, picking up his parachute. He had been testing a plane when it was shot down by a Zero and he had parachuted to safety in blue coveralls with a red bandanna in the pocket. The report was of Japanese paratroops in blue overalls with red emblems.

A little later, Commander Layton had a call from Commander Rochefort, the head of radio intelligence. He could not help with the location, but he said he did know that the flagship of the Japanese force was the carrier *Akagi*.

How did he know? demanded Layton.

Because the radiomen knew the "fist" or sending technique of the *Akagi* radio operator, and it was he who had been sending signals to the aircraft attacking the base.

That information was of no use to Admiral Kimmel, who wanted to make some decisions. He consulted with Captain McMorris, who was sure the Japanese ships had come up from the south and were lying south of Oahu. Kimmel ordered Admiral Halsey, who was not far away, to begin a search. Halsey was hampered because most of his dive-bombers were either in Oahu, shot down by the Zeroes, or on their way, but he began to search in the area indicated. All that he found there was water. Four of the B-17s soon managed to get off from Hickam air base and they went south to search. They found the cruiser *Minneapolis*. She sent a message: "No carriers in sight."

The message was garbled in transmission and arrived at Pearl Harbor as "Two carriers in sight," so Halsey was sent off again on a wild goose chase.

Admiral Wilson Brown's task force was also south of Oahu, and that afternoon as it steamed north, it was spotted by a PBY patrol plane returning from Midway. Thinking this was the Japanese task force, the PBY bombed and hit one of Admiral Brown's cruisers to add to the damage and confusion of the day.

When the first wave of Japanese attacked Pearl Harbor, the second wave was about halfway between the carrier force and the American base, fifty-four high-altitude bombers at 11,500 feet, split into three groups, one bound for Hickam Field to complete the destruction of the air facilities there, and two other groups bound for the Kaneohe Naval Air Station and Ford Island, the little airfield of the carrier planes.

At 10,000 feet were the dive-bombers — seventy-eight of them in all — organized into four groups. Their primary task would be to find ships in the harbor and wreck as many of them as possible.

Above the bombers flew thirty-five Zero fighters whose job was to protect the bombers, intercept American fighters, and strafe the airfields at Wheeler Field and the seaplane harbor and flying boat ramps of the Kaneohe air station.

Just at about the time that Commander Layton was worrying about the source of the Japanese attacks, the second wave struck.

One group of planes this time devoted their efforts to Bellows Field, where one of the incoming B-17s from the West Coast had landed. Nine planes strafed the B-17 that had already been wrecked in crash-landing. Two of the American fighters were shot down as they tried to take off.

The high-level bombers concentrated on the

hangars and shore installations at Kaneohe and wrecked a number of PBYs inside the hangars. One Zero fighter, strafing, was hit by a Browning automatic machine gun, and crashed into a road near the married officers' quarters. One more Zero was destroyed, but by the time the Japanese finished with Kaneohe, it was a real wreck. Three patrol bombers that were off on patrol escaped unharmed, six of those on the ground or in the water were damaged, and twenty-seven were destroyed. For the moment, at least, Kaneohe was out of commission.

At Wheeler Field some of the American fighters had begun to get into the air. Zeroes knocked two of them down as they were taking off. Lieutenant Kenneth Taylor shot down one or two Japanese planes, and Lieutenant George S. Welch shot one Zero off Taylor's tail. Then that particular group of Japanese fighters who were attacking Wheeler turned around and headed back for the rendezvous point to return to their carrier.

Sixteen other fighters headed for Hickam to strafe and protect fifty-four horizontal bombers heading that way. The leader of these fighters made one low-level pass over Hickam Field, and then climbed high, for this pilot's second duty was to assess the damage done to the American base and report to Commander Genda as the second strike was in progress so Genda could make some decisions about a third strike.

This fighter commander reported that heavy damage had been inflicted and gave no details.

The Japanese high-level bombers came in. The pilots of these planes were not as experienced as the bomber pilots of the first wave, but they did their job well, nonetheless. They also faced much more antiaircraft fire than the first wave had received, and many of the planes were well sprinkled with flak holes as they flew in to bomb.

At Hickam Field, they scored direct hits on Hangar 13, Hangar 15, and the mess hall, where they killed all the Chinese cooks who had taken shelter there.

The dive-bombers faced very heavy antiaircraft fire and so reported back to the *Akagi*. Commander Genda decided right then that if he was to call for a third strike, the torpedo bombers would stay aboard the carriers. The Pearl Harbor defenses were becoming stronger all the time.

By the time the dive-bombers reached Pearl Harbor the clouds of smoke from battleship row obscured much of the base. Down below the battleship *Nevada*, with a huge hole in her bow, moved past the overturned *Oklahoma*. The water was filled with oil and debris. The bombers singled out the *Nevada* and five bombs hit her. Before she could be beached the fore part of the ship was wrecked. Her casualties were 3 officers and 47 men killed and 5 officers and 104 men injured.

At ten o'clock the *Oglala*, which had been hard hit in the first raid, capsized and sank. The repair ship *Vestal* was moved to Aiea and beached.

The destroyer *Blue* got underway and started

out of the harbor. Her antiaircraft gunners were firing and brought down at least one Japanese plane.

Looking for targets, the dive-bombers found the cruiser *Raleigh*, which had been torpedoed in the first attack, and they dropped a bomb on her and then one pilot strafed the ship. One bomber dropped a bomb that struck the pier about 15 feet from the cruiser *Honolulu* and did some damage. That same bomb did some damage to the cruiser *St. Louis*, which was moored near the *Honolulu*, but the *St. Louis* got up steam and got underway.

By this time the Japanese bombers had run out of bombs and had gone back to strafe the airfields again. The last of the midget submarines then got into action, firing two torpedoes at the *St. Louis*, both of which missed, and the submarine popped to the surface. The gunners of *St. Louis* were firing at the submarine and thought they sank it.

As the Japanese moved, so did Lieutenants Welch and Taylor, who had landed at Wheeler Field and regassed and rearmed their planes in a respite between attacks. Over Barber's Point, the two American pilots ran into some Japanese planes and began shooting. In the end they were credited with seven enemy planes destroyed, four from the first raid and three from the second.

Some of the Japanese bombers and fighters came down over Hickam Field once they had exhausted all their bombs and continued to strafe, mostly aiming for the B-17s, several of which they damaged further.

But the second wave was more expensive for the Japanese, because the Americans were finally getting their defenses up, and the raid cost the enemy six fighter planes and fourteen dive-bombers.

Up above the mess of Pearl Harbor, Commander Fuchida's bomber was still circling, now badly damaged by antiaircraft fire. He assessed the damage done to the Americans: eight battleships, three light cruisers, three destroyers, and four auxiliary ships either sunk or damaged. Eighteen vessels in all knocked out of action by this attack. The U.S. Navy had also lost thirteen fighters, twenty-one scout bombers, forty-six patrol bombers, three utility planes, two transports, and two training planes, besides the five *Enterprise* carrier planes shot down by American guns and the enemy.

The army air force had taken a very bad pasting, with four B-17s lost, twelve B-18 bombers lost, two A-20 bombers, thirty-two P-40s, twenty P-36s, four P-26s, and two OA-9 aircraft. Damaged planes numbered eighty-eight pursuit planes, six reconnaissance aircraft, and thirty-four bombers.

American casualties were high: 2,400 navy, army, marines, and civilians killed, and 1,178 wounded. All this had been done at a cost to the Japanese of twenty-nine planes, one large submarine, and five midget submarines, with all their crews except Ensign Sakamaki, who washed up on the north shore of Oahu that day and became a prisoner of war.

Chapter 12

Admiral Nagumo

Admiral Nagumo was very nervous. As he and Admiral Kusaka and the others of the staff stood on the flag-bridge of the *Akagi* and watched the black dots that were the returning aircraft of the first strike, Nagumo's basic emotion was not elation that he had won a signal victory, but relief that he had not lost any carriers and very few aircraft.

From the outset, Nagumo had opposed the Pearl Harbor attack as too dangerous, and he had not lost his fear. Now his fears of failure were compounded by the worsening of the weather. The returning planes were flying into high seas and tricky winds that would make landings difficult. It was just another worry, added to the many that troubled Admiral Nagumo.

As Commander Fuchida's plane returned toward the carriers, he was already thinking of the third strike they should launch that afternoon. He had looked over the submarine base, which was undamaged, and the fuel tank area, where the Americans kept the oil and gasoline that had to be shipped into Hawaii from the American main- land. He had looked over the dry docks and repair facilities, and it had occurred to him that the ca- pabilities of Pearl Harbor as a naval base had not been touched, although the fleet had been hit and the airfields blasted. But he also knew that it would not take much time to repair the runways and to replace the aircraft of the air forces. If the ship facilities and the fuel supplies were de- stroyed, a really hard blow would have been struck against the Americans, and they would not be able to use Pearl Harbor as a naval base for many months.

There was no question in Commander Fuchida's mind, then, but that another air strike or perhaps two were in order to finish the job well begun that morning.

As the flying officers came in to the deck of the flagship *Akagi*, they reported to Air Officer Masuda for debriefing. The air officer had set up a blackboard on the flight deck near the bridge structure. As each officer reported, he was ques- tioned and his story of the damage was entered on the blackboard. Commander Genda came down to the flight deck a few times, eager for the final results as seen by the fliers. The second time he came down, quite a number of the pilots were on hand, and they pressed him to stage another attack. He was noncommittal.

At this time, another meeting of quite a different nature was in progress, at the White House in Washington. There, President Roosevelt had gathered together Secretary of War Stimson, Secretary of the Navy Knox, Secretary of State Hull, Chief of Naval Operations Stark, and Army Chief of Staff Marshall for a war conference, the first they held in World War II. President Roosevelt was issuing a barrage of orders, grounding private aircraft, renewing guard for military installations, and rounding up Japanese and German aliens.

The President knew that the results of Pearl Harbor were tragic, but in another sense they were welcome to him. For months he had labored under the shadow of American isolationism, trying to strengthen American defenses and assist the British in the war effort he knew was essential to control the march of fascism. Now, for the first time, his enemies had served him well, silencing once and for all the isolationists who had claimed that Roosevelt was leading them to a war that no one wanted. Now the war had been forced on America by the Japanese.

Roosevelt that afternoon decided that he would ask Congress next day for a Declaration of War against Japan. Soon he was on the transatlantic telephone conferring with Prime Minister Winston Churchill, learning of the Japanese attack on northern Malaya that same day, and agreeing that they would both make declarations of war against Japan.

It was four o'clock in the morning in Manila when the word of the Pearl Harbor attack began to seep through the naval and army commands. Admiral Hart had been awakened from a sound sleep to hear the news. General MacArthur had also learned and within the first hour he had a telephone call from the army war plans office in Washington, warning him that he should expect an attack at any time.

At 4:00 A.M. the air commander in the Philippines, Lt. General Lewis H. Brereton, put his aircrews on standby alert and asked permission to send his B-17s on a preemptive strike against the Japanese Formosa airfields. Had this been done, the Japanese planes would have been caught on the ground, but MacArthur refused to allow Brereton to act. Seven hours later that failure brought about total disaster to the air force in the Philippines, when the Japanese naval air force struck in great strength and caught the B-17s on the ground.

Commander Fuchida started back for the flagship *Akagi* with photographs of the damage done at Pearl Harbor. He counted four battleships sunk and three badly damaged. The airfields, he noted, had been efficiently destroyed as operational bases for the present.

It was nearly noon when the RCA messenger

188

carrying the war warning from General Marshall arrived at Fort Shafter with the message, and it was a long time before it was finally decoded. By that time it was not only useless, it was a grim reminder that Washington had not done its job and the army and navy commands at Pearl Harbor were the victims.

Commander Fuchida's plane was the last to board the *Akagi* that day and did not arrive until almost noon. Commander Fuchida rushed to the bridge of the carrier to report to Admiral Nagumo.

Instead of pleased congratulations he faced two questions from the worried Nagumo: Was the American fleet badly enough damaged that it would be out of operation for six months? Where were the American carriers?

Commander Fuchida said that he felt the damage to the fleet had been adequate to keep it out of action for six months, but that he had no idea where the American carriers were located. He brushed by the question. The thing to do now, he said enthusiastically, was to launch another strike and smash the Americans' oil storage and dockyard facilities. That way they would know that even if the carriers came back the fleet would not be able to operate out of Hawaii for a long time.

He and Genda had ordered the planes to be refueled and rearmed and ready for departure on another mission. Fuchida then went to the briefing room, where the pilots were continuing their attack reports.

But on the bridge of *Akagi*, Admiral Nagumo was having many thoughts about the whole situation he faced. He had done what he had been ordered to do, he said, he had attacked Pearl Harbor and protected the navy's flank so the American fleet could not interrupt the southern operations against Malaya and the Dutch East Indies.

He had done all he could do, said Admiral Nagumo.

Commander Genda disagreed. He and Fuchida both urged another air strike to knock out the Pearl Harbor bases definitely.

But where were the American carriers? asked Admiral Nagumo, again.

What if they came swooping down on him now, when his planes were off on another air strike that might not produce very much? If he stuck around here, he was risking three-quarters of the Japanese Combined Fleet's strength to wipe out port facilities. And they could expect higher losses. Only nine planes had failed to return from the first strike, but the second strike had cost twenty planes. A third strike must be even more costly as the American defenses were gotten into shape.

Also, Nagumo argued, he was now within range of American land-based air forces, and no one knew what might happen.

He was growing more nervous every minute.

Nagumo's chief of staff, Admiral Kusaka, took the admiral's side. Fuchida came to protest the decision not to attack again and was silenced. One by one the Nagumo staff came around to the side of their admiral. Instead of the council of victory that had been expected, the talk on the *Akagi* bridge sounded more like a council of despair. The Nagumo staff and the Admiral were now worried about the safety of their carrier force and aircraft, not about inflicting damage on the enemy.

Who could prove that the Americans did not have enough planes left on the land to launch an attack against the carriers?

No one.

And where were the American carriers?

Fuchida and Genda had to admit that the American carriers undoubtedly would now begin looking for the Japanese task force. This fact impressed Nagumo very much, and very negatively. It appealed to all his fears.

He asked Genda what he thought of the possibility of an enemy strike against the Japanese force.

Let the enemy come, said Commander Genda. If they did come, then the task force would shoot down their planes.

But that sort of argument did not affect Nagumo except to make him ever more fearful. The responsibility was his, not theirs.

Fuchida left the bridge, disgusted and heartsick at the timidity. Genda took over the argument. He was not satisfied with the damage done, he warned.

Japan had the chance of a lifetime to damage

the Pacific Fleet. If they would only stay and finish the job.

Genda did not advocate another attack that day. The aircraft had already been rearmed to meet an attack from ships at sea, in case the enemy carriers showed up. Let it remain that way. Let them wait, and let them find the American carriers. Let them stay in the area for two or three days to see what happened, and run down the enemy carriers as they appeared.

Nagumo considered the course. It went against all he believed, for his basic emotion was fear that he would overreach his capability and sacrifice one or more of the carriers — needlessly as it now seemed, since he had already achieved a victory over the American fleet and his officers said it would be out of action for six months.

What Genda now wanted was for Nagumo to send out scout planes and find the American carriers, while bringing down the tankers from the north and refueling and preparing for more action. What should be done now was to find the American carriers and destroy them, one by one, then go back and hit Pearl Harbor again on the way to the Marshall Islands, hit Pearl Harbor hard, destroy the fuel and repair facilities, and return to Japanese waters knowing that they had pulled the teeth of the enemy fleet.

In the face of the younger officers' hopes for a total victory, which they saw as achieved in one or two days of continued action, was the almost united view of the Nagumo staff, which wanted to play it safe and go home with what they had.

When this word came to Admiral Ugaki, Admiral Yamamoto's chief of staff, he characterized Nagumo as like the thief in the henhouse, who takes fright and runs off with a chicken or two when he could have the whole coop. He asked Admiral Yamamoto to order Nagumo to continue the action, but this Yamamoto refused to do. He also felt that Nagumo was chickenhearted, but he respected the right of the officer in command on the scene to make the decisions, no matter how much he disagreed, and he would not interfere with Nagumo.

Nagumo had to make up his mind; no, that was not really true. His mind had been made up from the beginning. He wanted to take the easy way, with the least danger to the striking force. They had achieved a victory beyond the furthest dreams of any but Yamamoto already, and Nagumo and his staff were not willing to go further. Nagumo vacillated, but his staff was strong and steady on the subject. They must return and go home now, said Admiral Kusaka.

He remembered, as did Admiral Nagumo, how much the Naval General Staff had disliked the Yamamoto plan from the beginning. He remembered that the basis on which they had gotten the six carriers instead of the four originally authorized was that they would all be made available immediately after the Pearl Harbor operation for use in the southern waters to support the Malaya and Dutch East Indies operations.

Admiral Nagumo and his staff had already forgotten what Admiral Yamamoto had told them; this was a great gamble and they should be prepared to lose a third of their force if necessary to accomplish the aims. They had accomplished it all so far without a scratch to the ships and a minimal loss of aircraft. Instead of considering the resources he had left and the damage they could inflict on the enemy, Nagumo and his staff were now considering their own safety and determined not to risk the task force at all.

Nagumo and Kusaka said to themselves that they had achieved 80 percent of what they wanted, and the other 20 percent was not worth the risk. But Genda and Fuchida said that the other 20 percent was the difference between success and basic failure. Nagumo could not see that in any sense he was failing by refusing to finish the job. So he persisted in his desire to leave the scene, his staff backed him, and the aviators, Genda and Fuchida and the flight leaders, were overwhelmed by the determined timidity of their superiors.

Kusaka was very pleased. He had opposed the whole operation from the beginning, but he had given his word to Yamamoto once the orders were given that they would be obeyed and the strike would be carried out. Now it had been carried out, and what was wanted by others was more than the call of duty, a risk to win a real victory rather than a partial one, and Kusaka was not interested. He wanted to get the carriers back to

Japan, where they could join in what he saw as the primary operation, the drive south.

And the admirals had their way.

The airmen asked Genda for an explanation of what they saw as a wrongheaded decision; Genda gave them three reasons:

1. The attack had achieved its expected results.
2. A second attack would bring new risks to the task force.
3. They did not know where the American carriers were.

Commander Genda dutifully made the excuses for Admiral Nagumo, but privately he called Nagumo a "miscast misfit" and lamented the fact that they had not been given either Admiral Ohnishi or Admiral Yamaguchi, both aggressive airmen, to command the operation. It was all the fault of the naval ministry, said the young officers, for putting this power into the hands of a man who was basically a "battleship admiral," and who did not understand the basics of carrier warfare.

And so that afternoon, as the carriers were being made ready for another attack, the order came down from the Nagumo bridge.

"Preparations for attack canceled," said the signal flags, and they were followed by others that announced the flagship's intention to retire to the northwest.

Commander Fuchida was just grabbing a bit of

late lunch when he learned all this. He rushed to the bridge, saluted Admiral Nagumo, and asked, "Why aren't we attacking again?"

Nagumo opened his mouth, but Admiral Kusaka answered, "The objectives of the Pearl Harbor attack have been achieved. Now we must prepare for other operations ahead."

Fuchida saluted and turned on his heel, unable to speak for frustration and anger.

And so the striking force began to retire. Still this was not quite the end of the story. . . .

Chapter 13

Aftermath at Pearl

In Honolulu, just a few miles from Pearl Harbor, the initial Japanese attack created no stir at all. The people of the city were used to strange doings at Pearl Harbor and on the west side of the island, where the navy and the army conducted training and maneuvers. It was not until nine o'clock that morning, when the first attack was nearly spent, that radio station KGMB broadcast the news that the Japanese had attacked. "This is the real McCoy," said the announcer. And then people began to believe that the rumors they had been hearing were true.

At the Japanese consulate, the early arrivals milled about, not knowing what to believe. Only when a reporter from the *Honolulu Star Bulletin* arrived with a copy of the Extra announcing

WAR! OAHU BOMBED BY JAPANESE PLANES

did the consulate staff realize that the attack was in progress, and then the staff began burning papers.

In midmorning, the FBI arrived and carted off many documents for the intelligence office at fleet headquarters.

President Roosevelt had just finished lunch in the Oval Office when Secretary Knox telephoned and told him about the Pearl Harbor attack. The Japanese ambassadors had not yet delivered their final message to Secretary Hull, and Hull was not sure whether or not he should receive them under the circumstances. Roosevelt told him to receive them, but to say nothing about Pearl Harbor.

So when Admiral Nomura and Ambassador Kurusu gave Hull their final message, the Secretary of State received them coldly, commented on the nature of their message, which he termed a pack of lies, and dismissed them. Admiral Nomura did not then know that the Japanese Navy had already attacked Pearl Harbor and did not find out until he returned to his home later in the afternoon. He was profoundly shocked, particularly at the position into which he had been put by his government.

Secretary of War Stimson was having a late lunch when he learned the news. He had a feeling of relief that the crisis had come, and in a way that it would unite Americans. In spite of the fact that the Pearl Harbor strike was a catastrophe, he welcomed its implications, for it put an end to the bickering about a war that he found inevitable.

Army Chief of Staff Marshall was having lunch when the news came. He hurried back to his office, where he remained until 3:00 P.M. when he had an appointment with President Roosevelt.

Commander Laurance Safford awakened from a sleep of exhaustion, engendered by all the strain of the past few days, to learn this his worst fears had been realized. He decided to stay at home. If he encountered either Admiral Noyes or Admiral Stark, he felt he would have murdered them right then for their refusal to let him warn Pearl Harbor and the other points that the Japanese were going to attack.

Secretary Hull stayed at the State Department until 3:00 P.M. and then went to the White House to join General Marshall and the President and several other advisers. Admiral Stark stayed at the navy department and kept relaying the bad news from Hawaii to the White House by telephone.

President Roosevelt telephoned Governor Poindexter in Hawaii and was talking to him when Poindexter suddenly announced that the second wave of bombers had just appeared and was working over Oahu.

President Roosevelt and General Marshall discussed the Philippines, and Marshall told the President that he had warned General MacArthur and MacArthur could be expected to take the necessary precautions against surprise in the Philippines.

The White House meeting broke up shortly and the various advisers went their own ways. Secretary Hull went back to the State Department, where he presided over a meeting of his own.

On the street in front of the White House and around Lafayette Park, several hundred people gathered to show their anger and frustration over the Japanese attack. They continued to come and go all afternoon and evening, with police urging them to disperse, but gently.

At around eleven o'clock that morning, Hawaii time, the destroyer *Ward* had used up all her depth charges, bombing what appeared to be many submarine contacts. Just after then, with the *Monaghan* and other destroyers now outside and sharing the work load, Lieutenant Outerbridge took the *Ward* inside the harbor, went to the ammunition depot, and renewed the supplies of depth charges. This time Lieutenant Outerbridge took aboard all the depth charges the ship could carry. By three o'clock that afternoon they were back outside, searching again for enemy submarines. They continued all day and evening to make contacts.

The afternoon of December 7, 1941, Admiral Kimmel and his staff were awaiting another strike by the Japanese when they had word of the first Japanese action against Guam, an air raid by planes from Saipan, which sank the naval ship *Penguin* in Apia Harbor. Shortly afterward came the word that Wake Island had been hit by the Japanese too, and seven of the new fighters delivered by Admiral Halsey had been destroyed. The *Pan American Clipper*, which had stopped over at Wake, had escaped and was on its way to Midway. The pilot radioed that he saw a Japanese cruiser and several destroyers that were heading for Wake. So it was apparent that the Japanese attack in the Pacific was general, and that worse news could be expected.

It was not long in coming. The news of heavy air raids on Hong Kong and the bombing of Singapore came next. From Shanghai came the word that the gunboat *Wake* had been captured. Then came word of two bombing attacks on the Philippines, and still MacArthur would not loosen the hands of his air commander to make retaliatory strikes. By late afternoon, the question in the Philippines was moot, for the Japanese had come to the Clark Field complex and had virtually wiped out American air power in their air raids.

It was midafternoon by the time that Commander Layton was able to tell Admiral Kimmel that the Japanese attackers had come from the north. The information came from the pilot's compartment of a downed Japanese plane. The pilot's plot board had been saved, and it showed the plane's course from the carrier force more than two hundred miles north of Oahu, and the course he should fly to get back, if he had been so lucky as to make it. But by this time the Japanese task force was already moving back out of range of American carriers.

Kimmel's orders to Task Force 8 were to search for the enemy. One of the Japanese submarines intercepted the message and warned Admiral Nagumo that the enemy was searching for him. But they were not looking in the north, they were looking to the south. One of the pilots of the B-17s remembered that he had seen Japanese planes coming from the north that morning, and he tried to interest people at air force headquarters in that information. But no one listened. "They seemed more interested in fitting liners inside helmets," the pilot remarked.

At about 1:00 P.M., Hawaii time, the Japanese striking force turned back north at 26 knots. Admiral Nagumo was worried again, this time lest the American carriers find his force. At just after five o'clock that evening, Nagumo ordered the ships to battle stations, and set up a combat air patrol that would go out at dawn 360 degrees in full circle and travel out to 300 miles around the carrier force.

That night the Japanese force made itself ready in case of discovery of the American carriers. Commander Genda prepared the level bombers ready for torpedoing and dive-bombing the next day.

Commander Fuchida told all officers to develop their attack photos for study of damage done to the American fleet. Planes from the other five carriers brought all their photos to the flagship, where the air intelligence officers studied them half the night. On the morning of December 8, Nagumo sent the light cruiser *Chikuma* and a destroyer to meet the supply group at the rendezvous point. The ships refueled and then brought the tankers down to join the fleet.

On December 8 in Tokyo, Imperial General Headquarters proclaimed that a state of war existed between Japan and the United States and British Empire.

In Washington, on the evening of December 7, all the members of the Roosevelt cabinet assembled in the White House Oval Office. President Roosevelt gave his cabinet members a précis of the events of the day and drew a parallel with the cabinet meeting of President Lincoln on the eve of the Civil War.

That night Secretary Stimson suggested that the President also declare war on Germany the next day when he spoke to Congress, but Roosevelt refused. He said that this would play into the hands of the isolationists. And besides, he knew from intercepts of Japanese coded messages that Foreign Minister von Ribbentrop had promised the Japanese ambassador to Berlin that Germany would declare war on the United States.

President Roosevelt made a point of inviting the Democratic and Republican leaders of Congress to this meeting, and they came in a little later. Roosevelt again catalogued the day's events.

The Congressional leaders tended to be caustic in the extreme. Senator Tom Connally charged that the army and the navy had been asleep at the switch, and he harried Secretary Knox because the navy did not "do anything " to the enemy that made the attack. Why were the ships all crowded together in Pearl Harbor, he wanted to know.

Had not Secretary Knox just two weeks earlier said that America could defeat the Japanese navy in two weeks?

Where were the American patrols, that they let the Japanese through to attack?

Finally the Congressional delegation left, still with many questions in the minds of the members, and much dissatisfaction with the conduct of the administration. But when they left, they agreed on one thing: from this day it would not be politics as usual. Senator McNary and other Republican leaders promised that whatever President Roosevelt did in this crisis, the country would be solidly behind him.

Later, that night, President Roosevelt had his latest shock, the news that in spite of all the warnings, General MacArthur had allowed himself to be surprised in the Philippines and that most of the American air force there had been wiped out in the day's Japanese air raids.

Next morning, Monday, the fire fighters at Pearl Harbor were still working to put out the blazes started by the Japanese attack. Rescue parties were still working among the battleships, trying to rescue men trapped inside the steel hulls. One by one the sounds of tapping stopped, the air supplies ran out, and the men inside the steel hulls suffocated or drowned.

That Monday morning, Admiral Kimmel assembled his staff of the Pacific Fleet to discuss the offensive measures he wanted to undertake. On balance, the disaster at Pearl Harbor had not seemed quite so disastrous. Kimmel had the two task forces, *Enterprise* and *Lexington*, at hand, and they could be sent out immediately. The carrier *Saratoga* was moving toward Pearl Harbor at that moment from the West Coast, to add to the offensive strength of the fleet. Kimmel also had nine heavy cruisers, all but two of the fleet's light cruisers, and all but three of the fleet's destroyers with which to work.

That morning, Admiral Wilson Brown's Task Force 12, built around the *Lexington*, was chasing after a rumor that the Japanese had attacked Johnston Island, but that rumor was dispelled by afternoon. North of Oahu, Rear Admiral Milo F. Draemel's light cruisers and the heavy cruiser *Minneapolis* were chasing the Japanese, fruitlessly as it turned out. Southwest of Oahu, Admiral Halsey was still looking for the Japanese, which Captain McMorris thought were down there, but that evening Task Force 8 came into Pearl Harbor, refueled, and then went out again. This time, Halsey caught a fish: the Japanese submarine *I-70*, which the task force sank with a great deal of satisfaction.

On December 8, President Roosevelt spoke to a joint session of Congress in the House of Representatives, where he characterized the events of December 7:

"Yesterday, December 7, 1941 — a date which will live in infamy — the United States was suddenly and deliberately attacked by the naval and air forces of the Empire of Japan. . . ."

Congress passed the war resolution then, with a single dissenting vote.

In Washington, the navy department, which had so completely missed the signs of impending disaster earlier in the month, now panicked completely. Admiral Turner's war plans division, which had been riding so highly and mightily over the Office of Naval Intelligence, now completely misread the signals from the Pacific and warned of a new impending attack on Pearl Harbor. The warning came on December 9, and it indicated that this second raid would be the forerunner to an attempt to occupy Midway, Maui, and Hawaii islands. Admiral Stark, who sent the nervous warning, advised that Pearl Harbor should refrain from any activity except for patrol craft, naval aircraft, and submarines, and that these should limit themselves to movement at times when there was no danger of Japanese attack.

ONI, on the other hand, had correctly assessed the Pearl Harbor raid as a "hit-and-run affair" and suggested that the Japanese were going back to their original objective, which was the conquest of the South Pacific.

In Japan, aboard the Combined Fleet flagship *Nagato* on this second day, Admiral Ugaki lamented Nagumo's decision to withdraw.

"In a situation where we lost only thirty planes, the most essential thing is to exploit the achieved results of the attack," he said. And Nagumo had sacrificed all that.

The senior staff officer of the Combined Fleet, Captain Kuroshima, called together some of the junior members of the Combined Fleet staff that evening to discuss the idea of recommending to Admiral Yamamoto a second attack be staged against Pearl Harbor. Most of the younger officers agreed that it should be done, provided the enemy carriers could be located. But the staff members saw some problems. One was the necessity of issuing new orders if the attack was to be renewed, and this meant getting the word to the tankers and other support ships for the striking force. More important, from the point of view of the Yamamoto staff, was the negative attitude of Admiral Nagumo, which was well known aboard the *Nagato*. Given that attitude and the expected support of Nagumo's staff for Nagumo's actions, to order Nagumo back into action would create some serious morale problems.

The next morning, Captain Kuroshima summarized all this material for Admiral Yamamoto at a meeting of the Combined Fleet staff, and urged that Admiral Nagumo be ordered to make another attack on Pearl Harbor to finish the task. But although Admiral Yamamoto listened thoughtfully to the arguments, and personally agreed with them, he refused to order Nagumo to turn around.

His reasons were:

1. This time the element of surprise would be missing, so the losses would be higher, although the results would be still good. Also, they might be attacked this time by enemy carrier planes, which could cause the loss of one or more carriers.
2. No plan for a second attack had been devised, and it was too difficult to carry out a mission such as that one without a detailed plan.
3. Nagumo and his men had already exerted their utmost ability, and the fact that they did not want to make the attack meant that if they were forced to do it, it probably would not be successful.

So, on balance, as much as Yamamoto sympathized with the motivations of his junior staff men, he rejected their suggestion and refused to interfere with Nagumo's plan to retire.

But the young staff members had one minor triumph. Yamamoto agreed that Nagumo should take more action. On December 9 he issued Fleet Order No. 14 telling Nagumo that if the situation permitted, he was to stop by Midway and attack, destroying Midway as an American base of operations and as a submarine base.

When this order reached Admiral Nagumo's force by radio, it was greeted with dismay by all concerned. Nagumo did not like it for the same reasons he did not like the whole operation. Admiral Kusaka did not like it because he considered it a nuisance. Commander Genda did not like it because he felt that it would endanger the striking force without giving any commensurate good effects.

Meanwhile, the same sort of discussion was taking place at the Naval General Headquarters in Tokyo, where the staff members, once so much opposed to the Pearl Harbor operation, were fascinated by the success of it. Some of them wanted to make Nagumo take another crack at Pearl Harbor. Admirals Fukudome and Tomioka discussed the question with junior staff members, but in the end their decision was the same as Yamamoto's: Let Nagumo retire.

So Nagumo started home to Japan, with Commander Genda and other members of the expedition sure that a golden opportunity had been flung away by Nagumo's timidity. "He who controls Hawaii controls the Central Pacific," said Genda. Having failed to knock out Hawaii, he was certain that the Japanese would have to come back and do the job over again, if they were to win the war against the Americans.

On the way home, Commander Genda offered a new plan to Admiral Nagumo. Let them stop off at Truk and replenish supplies and planes and ammunition. After that, let them take on several regiments of army and navy troops, and then let them invade and capture Wake, Midway, and Johnston islands, thus establishing a basis for the capture of Hawaii — before the Americans could recover from the shock of Pearl Harbor.

At this same time the Naval General Staff was becoming more than lukewarm to the idea of capturing Hawaii. Admiral Fukudome and Admiral Tomioka talked about it with other officers. But Fukudome later decided the idea, although attractive, was not feasible because it would require 500,000 tons of shipping and a number of tankers that were needed just now in the operations in the south. Always, when other plans were mentioned, the Naval General Staff kept returning to the necessity of carrying out the plans in progress.

In the end, after much discussion, the plan of stopping Admiral Nagumo en route and sending him back to Hawaii was killed. Or, rather, it was put in abeyance. The Naval General Staff said it was really a good idea. It presented many problems, not the least of which was the fact that Hawaii was not self-sufficient and that if occupied, the Japanese would have to feed the populace as well as their garrisons. But there was much to be said for taking a piece of territory in mid-Pacific, which would keep the Americans off balance for the rest of the war and could serve as a springboard for other occupations. So the Hawaii plan was put aside, pending completion of the Southern Operation successfully, and the Naval General Staff turned its attention to the Philippines, the Dutch East Indies, and the South Pacific.

In the North Pacific the weather grew very rough on December 12 and continued to worsen on December 13. Several members of the crew of the carrier *Hiryu* were washed overboard and lost in the high seas. The *Akagi* and the other carriers pitched and tossed so violently that it was impossible to consider any air operations at the moment. Citing the weather, then, Admiral Nagumo called off the idea of an attack on Midway, which he did not want to make under any conditions. Admiral Ugaki was very much disappointed by Nagumo's refusal to do more, but Yamamoto still declined to interfere or to comment on Nagumo's behavior. So Nagumo's decision stood, and the striking force headed back toward Japan. At about that time, the Fourth Japanese Fleet was having some second thoughts about its invasion of Wake. The invasion force had been repelled in the first attempt, two destroyers lost, and the whole expedition thrown into confusion. It had headed back for the Marshall Islands to regroup and try again. Now, the Fourth Fleet appealed to Admiral Yamamoto for some carrier support of its operations against Wake, and Yamamoto agreed that they should have it. He sent a message to

Nagumo to send the Second Carrier Division down to help out the Fourth Fleet in its capture of Wake.

When that word came, Nagumo put aside any further consideration of Commander Genda's plan to stop at Truk, resupply, take on troops, and then attack Midway and Hawaii.

On December 16, then, Admiral Nagumo sent the heavy cruisers *Tone* and *Chikuma* and the camera *Soryu* and *Hiryu* and two destroyers to leave the formation and head for Wake to help the Fourth Fleet capture that American outpost. But how much help was the Second Carrier Division going to give? Not very much, as it turned out. Nagumo warned that the ships were low on fuel, ammunition, and supplies, so they would make a single air raid on Wake and then they would head for home waters.

Nagumo steamed back toward Japan, and on December 17 he sent his Battle Report No. 1 back to Japan. The Japanese estimates of ship damage were surprisingly accurate, although those of damage to aircraft were exaggerated and wide of the mark.

When this damage report reached the Combined Fleet, the first reaction was positive, pleasure at having struck a powerful blow at the enemy. But when the officers began to consider the actual facts, they realized that the Japanese attack had been less than successful. The submarine base remained. The repair facilities remained, the oil tanks remained, and Pearl

Harbor remained a major operating base for the Americans. The battleships had been dealt with, but the aircraft carriers and cruisers had not been. The Americans still had a formidable force that would have to be dealt with at some time. At the moment, however, it was almost certain that the Americans would not be able to interfere with the southern operations. And that was satisfaction enough for the naval headquarters in Tokyo, and acceptable to the Combined Fleet.

After the Pearl Harbor attack, the news from the Pacific and news coming to Pearl Harbor was more and more dismal. On December 10, Admiral Kimmel learned that the battleship *Prince of Wales* and the battle cruiser *Repulse* had been sunk by the Japanese off the Malaya coast, thus wiping out British naval power in the Pacific. At the same time came the reports of continuing Japanese assaults on the Philippines.

While digesting this bad news, Admiral Kimmel was planning offensive operations to start immediately. He requested from Washington the replacement of aircraft and assured Admiral Stark that he was about to move offensively. The loss of the battleships, he told Stark, meant that the war plan had to be revised drastically to depend on the cruiser and carrier force for offensive operations.

"These forces must be operated boldly and vigorously on the tactical offensive in order to retrieve our initial disaster."

Admiral Kimmel now proposed that he keep two of the three available carrier task forces at sea at all times, for search and strike operations, while the third task force guarded the approaches to Hawaii. The surviving battleships would have been of no use in such operations anyhow because they were not fast enough to keep up with the carriers and cruisers, so they were to be sent back to the West Coast for guard duty there. Their principal value would be to protect the ocean convoy route to Pearl Harbor.

Except for the carrier raids, then, the major effort against Japan would be to use the submarine force most effectively to strike at Japanese lifelines and oil supplies.

Guam fell to the Japanese on December 10. The question of Wake Island then became first on the agenda of the Pacific Fleet. Admiral Kimmel proposed to defend Wake Island against the expected Japanese assault. On December 11, Admiral Kimmel was making preparations to send relief forces to sea.

Meanwhile Secretary of the Navy Knox secured Presidential approval for a secretarial trip to Pearl Harbor, to find out the extent of the damage done to the Pacific Fleet and to affix the responsibility. On the afternoon of December 10, Secretary Knox and a party of civilians and naval officers set out for California, where they would take a flying boat to Pearl Harbor. Knowing that they were coming, Admiral Kimmel prepared himself for the worst; he fully expected to be relieved of command and made the goat for the Pearl Harbor attack.

General Short was also waiting for an army investigating team to come, but the army team's plane crashed in the California mountains and all were killed. The army investigation did not ever get started.

When Secretary Knox arrived, he signaled that this was anything but a pleasure or courtesy trip; he went directly to the Royal Hawaiian Hotel, where he was met by Admiral Kimmel and taken to Pearl Harbor, past the shambles of battleship row. The secretary visited hospitals, where he saw some of the badly burned survivors of the Japanese attack. He listened as Admiral Kimmel described the events. Kimmel wanted to talk about the salvation of Wake Island, but the secretary wanted to talk about the responsibility for the surprise. He was told that Pearl Harbor had been given no inkling of a Japanese threat to attack. One of Knox's aides, Captain Beatty, kept asking everyone at Pearl Harbor if they had received the navy's war warning of December 6, which was never delivered. Neither he nor the secretary seemed able to believe the real fact, that Washington had let Pearl Harbor be surprised.

The secretary's visit was a strain all the way around. After thirty-two hours, Secretary Knox and his party headed back for the mainland, he having first approved Admiral Kimmel's plan for the relief and protection of Wake Island.

Even as Secretary Knox's party was moving back toward Washington, the demands of Congress for some heads were beginning to be heard. And to add to the problem, army was blaming navy and navy was blaming army for the surprise by the Japanese.

On Wake Island the marines were fighting hard against the Japanese. As noted, the marines had repelled the first Japanese efforts to take the island. After three days of air raids, the Japanese tried to land their troops, coming in with two light cruisers, four destroyers, and four troopships. As they loaded their landing barges, the marine artillery opened up on them and sank the destroyer *Hayate*. They also damaged another destroyer and set a transport afire, and the Japanese abandoned the landing effort. In the fighting the marine aircraft sank another Japanese destroyer.

Admiral Kimmel then planned to use the relief of Wake Island as bait for the Japanese, to mount as powerful an offensive as he could. He proposed to use all three carrier task forces, to strike the enemy a hard blow when they sent back a stronger invasion force than before. Admiral Brown's task force would make a diversionary raid on Jaluit Atoll to pin down the enemy forces in the Marshalls. Admiral Halsey's task force would operate off Johnston Island as cover for Hawaii and support for the operation. The *Saratoga* task force would attack the Japanese in the Wake area, while the seaplane tender *Tangier*

216

came in to bring ammunition and supplies for the Wake garrison.

The plans for the relief of Wake were made, and they were awaiting the arrival of the *Saratoga* from the West Coast to be put into effect. Then, on the night of December 14, Secretary Knox returned to Washington and delivered to President Roosevelt a twenty-nine-page report on his findings in his "investigation" of the Pearl Harbor attack.

Knox reported on the enormous damage he had seen, and his assessment: that the surprise had been caused by the unreadiness of both the army and the navy commands at Pearl Harbor. But Secretary Knox also took account of the failure of Washington to give the Hawaii commands sufficient information.

Secretary Knox suggested that a board of inquiry be established to investigate the Pearl Harbor disaster. He also recommended that Admiral Kimmel be relieved, because his name was intimately connected with the disaster. But his biggest recommendation involved a shake-up of the whole navy command, because he recognized that Admiral Stark and the other admirals in Washington had let Pearl Harbor down badly. In order to do this and put the navy's house in order without creating too much trouble, Knox proposed that Admiral Ernest J. King be appointed to a new job, "Commander in Chief of the U.S. Fleet."

When this change was endorsed by President Roosevelt and made, it meant that the authority of Admiral Stark as chief of naval operations was ended, although temporarily he retained his post — a title that suddenly had become meaningless.

That change was not enough to satisfy those who demanded that the blame for Pearl Harbor be fixed on some personalities. And in the next few hours, it became apparent that Admiral Kimmel and General Short were to be delivered up as sacrifices to the politicians and the public, who must have scapegoats, who could not accept that fact that the whole nation had been surprised by its own unreadiness for war. The pressures were just too great, and so on December 16 the appointment of Admiral Chester W. Nimitz to be the new commander of the Pacific Fleet was approved at the White House. Kimmel was out, and Nimitz was in.

The responsibility of the army was as great as that of the navy, but General Marshall had President Roosevelt's confidence in a way that Admiral Stark did not, so the army high command escaped scot-free; neither Marshall nor General MacArthur, who had allowed himself to be surprised many hours after Pearl Harbor was known to him, received any criticism whatsoever. The heads of General Short and Admiral Kimmel were enough to assuage the demand for punishment of somebody. Now the nation could get down to the business of fighting the war to win.

Chapter 14

More Confusion

Ten days after the Pearl Harbor attack, Admiral Nagumo's striking force was heading home gratefully. The weather improved as they came closer to Japan. The patrol planes flew all day long to keep the task force alert to any dangers, for they had no information about the American carriers or about American submarines, which might be lurking anywhere. From time to time, sightings were recorded, but they were all imaginary; there wasn't a single American submarine in the Japanese line toward home.

Combined Fleet had some submarine trouble of its own, of another kind. Two Japanese submarines patrolling off Wake Island collided at night, and both of them sank. But the Fourth Fleet was making its preparations to attack Wake again, and this time to capture the island, so the fleet would not be disgraced.

The carriers of Carrier Division Two were

heading for Wake Island, and the rest of the Nagumo striking force was heading home on December 16, when a new bombshell was exploded at Pearl Harbor. Admiral Kimmel and General Short were summarily relieved of their commands that day and informed shortly afterward that they would have to bear the brunt of an investigation into the reasons for the surprise at Pearl Harbor. By this manner of announcing the investigation, President Roosevelt and the administration removed the onus from the Washington army and navy commands, where it surely belonged, and put it on the commanders in the field, men who had been kept in the dark by Washington about Japanese intentions and activities for the most part. Until that moment, and even afterward, for a little while Admiral Kimmel thought that he would be reassigned to war duty of some valuable nature. Admiral Stark so assured him. But then Stark did not know that he was also being held personally responsible for some degree of the damage, and that his own career had virtually come to an end. He would go to England for a time as a sort of supernumerary, but he would not again be employed in a vital command capacity.

After the surprise of the attack had ended, and the Pearl Harbor command began to pick up the pieces, in that first ten days after the attack, Admiral Kimmel was preparing to do battle with the enemy. His plans for the Wake Island relief, as noted, were much grander than they seemed; he was making ready to launch a major assault on the

Japanese to repay them in kind for the Pearl Harbor attack. That last day, Admiral Kimmel briefed Vice Admiral Frank Jack Fletcher, who had taken command of the *Saratoga* task force and was heading out from Pearl Harbor on December 16. Then Admiral Halsey's task force entered Pearl Harbor for replenishment, prepared to go out and fight, too.

The changeover of command was held on the afternoon of December 17; Vice Admiral William Pye, the second senior officer at Pearl Harbor, came from his flagship to fleet headquarters and took temporary control. Admiral Kimmel bade farewell to his staff and went to his quarters on Makalapa Heights to await new orders.

So what was Admiral Pye to do now that he was in temporary command? Not having the vaguest idea, having been convinced before the attack that the Japanese would never dare to attack Pearl Harbor, knowing virtually nothing about the situation or the enemy, Admiral Pye was inclined to do nothing, and so that is what he did. Why should he stick his neck out to follow the plans laid down by the now disgraced Admiral Kimmel to fight back and hit the enemy hard? In a few days, another admiral would be coming to take command of the Pacific Fleet. Let that admiral fight the battles. Let Admiral Pye simply hold the fortress of Pearl Harbor together in the interim.

Admiral Pye's reluctance to continue the Wake Island reinforcement mission was further extended by Rear Admiral Wilson Brown, who discovered that most of his antiaircraft ammunition was defective just as he was about to leave Pearl Harbor on the first leg of the mission.

Admiral Pye's justification for inaction was his concern lest he be sending the American forces into a trap, which could have been created by the dispatch of a large Japanese land-based air force to the Marshall Islands. The fact that this might have occurred was nothing but conjecture on Pye's part; it was what he feared might happen, but it was enough to justify his unwillingness to stick his neck out.

The fact was that it was the Japanese who were about to walk into a trap, the trap baited by Admiral Kimmel with the dispatch of the relief force for Wake Island. The Japanese were sending two carriers to Wake and four cruisers to help the Fourth Fleet with their capture attempt.

On December 19, Admiral Halsey's Task Force 8 steamed out of Pearl Harbor to go on guard of the western approaches to Hawaii. The next day the relief force under Admiral Fletcher approached the halfway point on its passage to Wake Island. Also on December 20, Admiral Wilson Brown decided it would be too risky for him to raid Jaluit or some point in the Marshalls, so he set out to raid Makin Island in the Gilbert chain instead. And at that point, the intelligence officers at Pearl Harbor had a highly inflated estimate of the Japanese strength in the Marshalls and Gilberts, which frightened Admiral Pye further.

At this point Admiral Pye decided he could not take any action that might possibly cause the loss of a carrier, so he ordered Admiral Brown to stop what he was doing and go north to support Fletcher, and he also ordered Fletcher to stop moving toward Wake and refuel. This, of course, delayed the approach to Wake Island, which is what Admiral Pye wanted to do.

Meanwhile from Wake Island came more calls for help and more information about air attacks on Wake, this time from carrier planes, which meant that the two carriers sent down by Admiral Nagumo had come within striking distance of Wake.

Admiral Pye then got the wind up, said he wanted only to protect Hawaii and did not care about Wake, and sent a radio message to this effect to Admiral Stark. Stark agreed completely. He did not want to stick out his neck either, and he said that Wake Island was a definite liability and should now be abandoned. Pye was then told that if he preferred to evacuate the garrison of Wake that would be all right, instead of defending the island. On the morning of December 22, Admiral Fletcher was just 600 miles north of Wake when Admiral Fletcher did what he liked best, fuel instead of fight. The fueling, which was totally unnecessary, took ten hours. If Fletcher had continued on course to Wake, he would have been in position the next day to smash the Japanese invasion force, which had just sailed from Kwajalein.

On the night of December 22, the marine garrison on Wake Island was still expecting the reinforcement it had been promised and was preparing to make a final stand the next morning while awaiting the assistance. Half the guns were knocked out but half were still firing. All their fighter planes were gone.

Just before 3:00 A.M. the Japanese barges arrived on the beach and began landing. The marines resisted in hand-to-hand fighting but by five o'clock the issue was in doubt and the Japanese were still pouring ashore. The reinforcements for Wake Island were nowhere to be seen.

At Pacific Fleet headquarters, Admiral Pye was vacillating. Captain McMorris, the plans officer, recommended that Fletcher attack and that Wilson Brown steam up to help him.

But Fletcher was still fueling, taking on fuel his ships did not need, avoiding battle. And he was more than 400 miles away from Wake, because he had stopped.

Admiral Brown was twice as far away, and Admiral Halsey was off Midway and too far away to help at all immediately.

But if Fletcher attacked and then Brown came up and Halsey moved, then the Japanese would be trapped on three sides, and the battle should be won.

Pye then began issuing conflicting orders. He first ordered Fletcher to take *Saratoga* forward and attack the Japanese. But no sooner had the order been received than it was countermanded.

Pye then ordered the seaplane tender *Tangier* into Wake, to evacuate the survivors. And half an hour later this order, too, was canceled, as Pye fidgeted.

At 9:11, Pye ordered Fletcher's and Brown's task forces to return to Pearl Harbor without fighting. A few minutes later he received the news of the Wake Island surrender to the Japanese. It was apparent that neither Pye nor Fletcher wanted to fight. Admiral Fitch, who did want to fight, felt constrained to obey the orders not to do so. Some of the fliers aboard the *Saratoga* nearly mutinied because of the timidity of their superiors.

So Admiral Pye and Admiral Fletcher superintended the American defeat at Wake Island, a defeat both unnecessary a unwanted. Worse, those two turned victory into defeat. Admiral Kimmel's plan came within a hair's breadth of working. Had it not been for the cowardice of those two admirals, a cowardice that was to be repeated by Admiral Fletcher at Guadalcanal, America could have enjoyed its first victory of the Pacific War and Wake would have been saved from the Japanese.

That day, the American government hierarchy was more concerned about assessing the blame for the Pearl Harbor attack than about winning the war. The administration's move was to stick the blame on the people at Pearl Harbor instead of the navy department in Washington. That day, the

Roberts Commission, led by Supreme Court Justice Owen J. Roberts, arrived in Honolulu to begin its star chamber investigation, an inquiry whose basic aim was to pin the blame on Admiral Kimmel and General Short, not to get at the facts. When the report was finally prepared, Admiral Standley, one of the members of the commission, wanted to make a minority report in protest, but was persuaded not to do so because such divisive, if justified, action might hurt the American war effort. Thus was the star chamber investigation allowed to end as it was intended to end, by pinning the blame for the Pearl Harbor attack where it did not belong, on the commanders in the field, who were not given the information to protect their commands by the navy and army in Washington, because the navy and army in Washington were playing promotion and power games.

The Roberts Commission investigation continued until January 9, 1942, when Admiral Pye was called as the last witness. The next day the commission returned to Washington, arriving on December 15 and finishing its work on January 23. That night President Roosevelt read the commission's report, and then gave the whole report to the American Sunday newspapers. So Americans were told that they had been let down by the Hawaii commands of the army and the navy. The reputations of General Short and Admiral Kimmel were tarnished forever, and it was not long before both officers were forced into retirement and lived for the rest of the war with the threat of disciplinary action against them if they protested their virtual conviction on these basically unfounded charges.

It was only after the war, when it was much too late to restore the careers of Admiral Kimmel and General Short, that the truth was allowed to come out. At that point, Admiral King summed up the reality of the situation that had come out of the Pearl Harbor attack:

"Admiral Kimmel was not asked the important questions, nor was he given the proper chance to speak for himself. In fact, he and General Short were 'sold down the river' as a political expedient."

Thus the real culprits, who certainly included Admiral Stark and Admiral Turner, got off scot-free. Stark was sent to England, where he moldered quietly away and was finally forgotten long before the war ended. Admiral Turner was sent to sea and rehabilitated himself by becoming the commander of amphibious operations in the Pacific, but he was not trusted again with a major area or headquarters command. And General MacArthur, who was responsible for the completely unnecessary surprise of American forces in the Philippines, was allowed to continue in command. Although thoroughly eclipsed in the first half of the war, he managed to make a comeback and returned to authority in the final days of the war, and ultimately supervised the Japanese occupation and the beginning of the war in Korea.

In fact, the Pearl Harbor problem persisted all through the war, and by 1945 it had become a political issue between Republican and Democratic parties, which is really where it ended. The military high commands of the army and navy, who bore the real responsibility, were never called to account for their dereliction and for the very good reason that the disaster at Pearl Harbor was really the national fault, and not that of any individual. America had grown fat and sloppy in the years of peace after 1918 and was disinclined to accept any international responsibilities. The army and the navy followed the national pattern, and their attitudes were narrow and self-serving in 1941. After Pearl Harbor, at first it was a question of vengeance — somebody had to be the scapegoat. After the war the question of justice was submerged in partisan politics. So the Pearl Harbor syndrome remained, and would remain, and the proof of that pudding was to come in the surprise of the American high command once more in June 1950, when the North Koreans attacked South Korea and once again the United States was completely unready for the shock.

Chapter 15

The Fleet Fights

As Christmas 1941 approached, Pearl Harbor was filled with gloom and loathing. The collapse of the Wake Island rescue mission had left most of the staff disappointed in their seniors, and it had also sapped what little confidence remained. Most of the junior officers of the fleet command were thoroughly disgusted with Admiral Pye and his timidity. Nothing was happening. The smell of defeat and frustration hung heavy in the air.

Most of the officers wanted to get out of the Pacific Fleet headquarters and get to sea, where they would at least have a chance to fight the Japanese.

Into this atmosphere on Christmas Day flew Admiral Chester W. Nimitz, fresh from Washington, his last news of the Pacific Fleet being that the relief of Wake Island had been authorized and that a fight was expected in which the Japanese would be hit hard.

When Nimitz arrived in his Catalina flying boat

that morning to land in the East Loch, his arrival was made grimmer by the sight of bodies still floating up from the wrecks of the battleships on battleship row and the stink of fuel oil that still covered half the harbor surface. Nimitz came in wearing civilian clothes and had to stand all the way to shore in the whaleboat that picked him up from the aircraft landing ramp because the whaleboat was greasy from fuel oil, the residue of rescue operations over the past few days.

Nimitz had a question.

"What about the relief of Wake?" he asked.

He was told then that the relief expedition had been called off. He asked no more questions. He went silent, and did not have anything else to say during the trip.

"A terrible sight, all these ships down," he finally said. And that was all he could force himself to say in the face of the dereliction of duty of the man who had succeeded Kimmel in the responsibility of command at a key moment, a responsibility Pye had been unwilling to shoulder.

In the next few days, Nimitz felt his way carefully among the dispirited members of the Pacific Fleet staff. He had very little to say, and no criticisms to make. He looked them all over carefully with his clear blue eyes, and if he was making judgments he was keeping them to himself just now.

The first week was spent assessing and watching and waiting. Then on December 31, Nimitz took command of the Pacific Fleet. As an old submariner he chose to take command on the deck of a submarine, perhaps because this ship represented his major offensive weapon of that moment. But in any event, all through the war the command ship of the Pacific Fleet remained from that moment a submarine. It became the symbol of Nimitz's operations.

Nimitz then told the Pacific Fleet staff, most of whom expected and wanted to be reassigned, that he wanted to keep them on duty with him. What he was doing in fact was fighting for time; not that he believed in all these men who had served Kimmel and some who had served Pye. In time he would begin replacing them with men he trusted, but for the moment he did not want change to muddy up the already oil-soaked waters of Pearl Harbor.

At the moment Admiral Nimitz had limited resources with which to work and a directive from Washington (one that Admiral King detested) that the European war was to take precedence over the Pacific war in terms of men and ships. This decision was engineered that Christmas week by Prime Minister Winston Churchill and the British chiefs of staff who came to Washington and argued persuasively that Hitler had to be beaten first, in the interest of preserving Britain and rescuing Europe, before attention was turned fully to the Japanese.

The first news to reach Pearl Harbor was bad news. King's first directive was given after the conference in Washington with Prime Minister

Churchill and the British warlords. Roosevelt had not taken much convincing to decide that the European war had to come first. King ordered Nimitz to hold the lines of communication to Midway and Australia, but otherwise to confine his efforts to raids against Japanese forward bases and to reinforce Samoa. That was all. There would be no counteroffensive for a while. The last chance had been lost at Wake Island, before Nimitz came into command.

Nimitz's greatest first task was to eliminate the defeatism that had soaked through Pearl Harbor. He began to do this by showing an air of quiet confidence. Very shortly the Pacific Fleet staff presented Admiral Nimitz with a program of carrier strikes against the Gilbert and Marshall islands. In addition to the carriers *Lexington*, *Enterprise*, and *Saratoga*, the Pacific Fleet was now to have the carrier *Yorktown*, which had been recalled from Atlantic duty.

Nimitz seized on this opportunity and planned an attack. On the evening of January 31, Rear Admiral Sukeyoshi Yatsushiro on Kwajalein gave a dinner party for his staff. Meanwhile Admiral Halsey's task force was speeding toward the Marshalls to make a raid. Early the next morning the raid came off, achieving complete surprise. The Japanese fought back vigorously, however, and one attacking twin-engined bomber tried to crash-dive the carrier *Enterprise* and caught a wingtip on the flight deck before it cartwheeled into the sea. It was a narrow escape for the carrier.

Also the cruiser *Chester* took one bomb hit from a Japanese plane.

The American aircraft attacked Kwajalein in waves, sinking several transports and damaging some shore installations. As a raid it was not much, but it served to release the feelings of the sailors involved and give the sense of fighting back. Meanwhile Admiral Raymond A. Spruance's cruisers attacked Wotje Atoll and the *Yorktown* carrier task force attacked Makin, Mili, and Jaluit.

No warships were sunk in these raids, but Admiral Yatsushiro was killed, and the Japanese were chagrined at having been caught asleep.

Most important from the American point of view is that the defeatism that had come after the attack at Pearl Harbor was partially wiped away. What remained of it would change only after some personnel changes were made at Pearl Harbor, but these were coming as Admiral Nimitz settled in and got to know the capabilities and weaknesses of the staff.

In February 1942, Admiral King became worried about the safety of Australia and pushed Nimitz into sending forces down to Australian waters to join in the defenses there. At the end of January he had ordered Nimitz to send a task force, and the only one available just then was Admiral Wilson Brown's *Lexington* force. All of the Cincpac staff opposed this move, but King was adamant. On February 6, he repeated the order, calling on Nimitz to take strong action to check what King saw as a dangerous Japanese advance in that region. Nimitz called a staff meeting, which backed his reluctance to send a force just then, and next day he advised King that to send the task force was most inadvisable. King became furious and ordered Nimitz to review the proposition of conducting offensive operations against the Gilberts, the Marshalls, and Wake Island.

Nimitz then sent Admiral Pye to Washington to reason with King. What Pye discovered was a full-scale war among the admirals. The subject was naval intelligence, and King and Admiral Turner were battling for control of it then, setting up his own men as the arbiters of naval intelligence operations.

In the midst of this Washington confusion, Admiral Halsey's task force sailed from Pearl Harbor on Valentine's Day 1942. Out on another raid. As it turned out, these early raids were very important in the American development of carrier warfare. Before December 7, there was no real carrier doctrine in the United States. Admiral Halsey knew as much as any commander about the niceties of carrier warfare, and he had a lot to learn. The carrier was a new weapon, developed between the two world wars, and the Americans had the least experience of any of the big powers. The Japanese had gained experience in the China war, and the British had gained experience in the European war, particularly with their successful raid on the Italian fleet at Taranto. But the Americans had to do it all. The American experience until the spring of 1942 had been confined to maneuvers over fourteen years.

On the raids conducted by Halsey, for example, he was learning to make optimum use of radar. He used it to locate his own aircraft after they set out from the carrier, and to correct their navigation while they were en route to the target. He learned the importance of incendiary bullets, and the need for leak-proof fuel tanks — all of these items had to be learned through experience. Another matter that received Halsey's serious attention was that of the need for many reserve pilots and aircrews for long carrier missions. It was asking too much of men to keep them at battle stations for perhaps twenty hours at a stretch and then to fly four- or five-hour missions, to return and be called upon very shortly afterward to fly search and patrol missions as well.

Halsey was learning and operating efficiently. Meanwhile Admiral Wilson Brown's task force was heading for a raid on Rabaul, the new big Japanese army and navy base established on New Britain Island. Admiral Brown's force was attacked by planes from Rabaul, which failed to get through the combat air patrol, and several were shot down. But surprise was lost and the Japanese returned to their own plans, which included troop landings and the capture of Lae and Salamaua on the New Guinea coast.

Meanwhile on February 24, Admiral Halsey made a raid on Wake Island that was largely ineffective, although it was called a huge success at Pearl Harbor.

After refueling, Admiral Halsey then turned to Marcus Island and made another raid. It too was successful, but very limited in scope. The major effect of these raids was to keep the Japanese high command off balance and to help restore American morale, even if militarily they accomplished very little.

In February and March 1942, the Pearl Harbor command fended off several Japanese nuisance bombing attacks, launched apparently from submarine-borne aircraft off the islands and by the big Kawanishi flying boats.

In March, Cincpac was alerted and concerned about Japanese movements in the New Guinea area. Admiral Wilson Brown's task force was still in that area, having joined with Admiral Fletcher's *Yorktown* Task Force to plan another assault on Rabaul. After a good deal of worrying over the problem of attacking, Admiral Brown finally sent his planes off over the 15,000-foot Owen Stanley mountain range of New Guinea to attack the Japanese forces bringing ships to Lae and Salamaua. The approach of the American planes over the mountain was concealed by rain squalls, and at 7:30 on March 9 the Americans attacked the Japanese flotilla. The assault created every bit as great a surprise to the Japanese as Pearl Harbor had done to the Americans. They sank four of the eighteen Japanese ships and damaged thirteen. It was a highly successful attack, and it forced Admiral Inouye to postpone the projected assault on Port Moresby from April until May. This raid, although virtually ignored at the time, was really the first major American counteraction to Japanese expansion in the Pacific.

In spring of 1942, Washington was understandably nervous because of the successful attack on Pearl Harbor of December. In the shakeup of naval intelligence in Washington, a great deal of information was knocked out of the intelligence trees from time to time. In the first few months of the year, Washington was forever getting the wind up and predicting new enemy strikes on Hawaii and Midway. One such prediction came on March 11. Like the others that spring, it proved to be erroneous, but it had caused a new alert at Pearl Harbor.

In April came the Doolittle raid, in which Admiral Halsey took the carriers *Enterprise* and *Hornet* to within 600 miles of the Japanese coast and launched a squadron of B-25 medium bombers that conducted a spectacular, although militarily insignificant, raid on Japan. The "stunt," as it was called at Pearl Harbor, had been opposed by many of Nimitz's staff, particularly by Rear Admiral Milo F. Draemel, whom Nimitz had inherited from Pye as chief of staff. Most of the planes would be lost, Draemel said, and that was the major concern. Draemel was quite right. All the B-25s were lost.

But Draemel was again exhibiting that defensive mentality that had brought about Pearl Harbor, and Nimitz, who recognized the spectacular nature of the operation at hand, still approved, because as he knew sometimes other considerations were more important than the purely military. And this was one of the times, with the Pacific Fleet still not recovered from Pearl Harbor, with military and civilian morale at low ebb, it was time that the United States "did something" to show a fighting spirit and give a forecast of the future.

And indeed, the Doolittle raid did all that it was supposed to do — it did a great deal to raise American civilian and military morale. It was needed just then more than ever, because at this time Bataan fell and the collapse of Corregidor was a little more than a month away.

By this time, General MacArthur had left the Philippines, which now became Japanese territory, and moved to Australia, to begin a campaign against the Japanese in the South Pacific. Admiral Nimitz was waiting for ships and for word to begin some offensive operations of his own. But the legacy of Pearl Harbor died hard, and in this spring of 1942 the American feeling in Hawaii was still defensive. Admiral King kept prodding Nimitz to take some sort of offensive action, just about any offensive action would satisfy him, because King above all others recognized the need.

In March, Admiral King asked Admiral Nimitz what he thought about subdivision of the Pacific Ocean into two major areas, one under command of Nimitz, and the other under the army command of General MacArthur. The whole American plan had been turned upside down by the collapse in the Philippines, occasioned by Washington's decision not to reinforce the Philippines. The first illustration was the decision to stop the convoy that was sent toward the Philippines in December and divert it to Australia. Australia was to be the army's new line of defense in the Pacific, and Nimitz was to defend the ocean areas and the Central Pacific. The real problem was that the eyes of the new Joint Chiefs of Staff organization were turned primarily toward Europe, and no one except Admiral King had given a great deal of concern to what was to be done in the Pacific.

By April, Admiral Nimitz knew from his increasing efficient radio intelligence organization at Pearl Harbor that the Japanese were planning new moves in the South Pacific, and he was trying to put together a force capable of opposing it successfully.

Imperial General Headquarters had authorized a new phase of the Japanese campaign in the south. It was to be the capture of British New Guinea and the investment of the Solomon Islands, to prepare for later assaults on Samoa, the French Pacific islands, Fiji, and then Australia. This authorization came from Imperial General Headquarters in January, and by April the planning was well along. Meanwhile, Admiral Yamamoto was planning a much more daring operation for June — the capture of the Midway atoll and the drawing out of the American fleet from Pearl Harbor for destruction at Midway.

So the next operations of the Imperial Navy were to be at Port Moresby, where the navy would lead the assault of the army forces and at the same time establish a seaplane base at Tulagi, a little island off Florida Island in the Solomons chain.

But in late March and early April the Americans did not know all this. Admiral Robert Theobald, making an estimate for Nimitz at Cincpac, said that the Japanese were probably going to move soon against Pearl Harbor again. Theobald recommended more defensive action, holding strong forces, perhaps two carrier groups and other capital ships within a thirty-six-hour run of Oahu, until the Japanese committed themselves. The defensive mentality was still operating at full strength. Nimitz did not like that advice, but as usual he sought a consensus of his staff, and they agreed that perhaps such an attack might come. But they also agreed that it was not about to come soon, and the Pacific Fleet could not be hamstrung with defensive plans all the time.

This attitude was certainly shared in Washington, particularly by the group of young aviators who were emerging to command status in these early days of the war. Admiral John Towers, the chief of the Bureau of Aeronautics, had many ideas about the future of carrier warfare and was looking forward to the day when the United States would have a carrier fleet of a dozen or more with which to develop an entirely new strategy of carrier operations.

Admiral Towers and the other aviators were restless under the continued management of the navy by the "battleship admirals." Particularly now that the American battleship fleet had been rendered inoperative, they saw the need for an entirely new strategy and war plan, and new faces to carry these out. Frank Jack Fletcher, for example, wore wings on his uniform, but they were more decorative than real; Fletcher had no real feeling for aviation, nor did most of the other admirals. Admiral Audrey C. Fitch was a rare exception, a real pilot. So was Admiral John McCain, who was going to the South Pacific to manage the land-based air force.

Even Halsey, although he was a qualified pilot, had not learned to fly until he was in his fifties, and therefore his whole attitude toward the navy and naval aviation was a little different from that of the pilot officers, who had come up through the ranks of aviation.

As the Japanese prepared to move forward and southward in their drive for empire, and Nimitz pondered over the best means that he could find to forestall such moves, Nimitz also had a whole group of other worries. Most important of these was the matter of the strategy that the Pacific Fleet would employ in the months to come as they tried to turn the war around with the limited resources they could expect.

One of the first moves in this turnaround had to be agreement on basic issues between Nimitz and Admiral King, who controlled basic naval operations. They had agreed to hold a series of meetings to discuss strategy and other affairs. The first of them was scheduled to be held at naval headquarters in San Francisco. So toward the end of April, Admiral Nimitz took a flying boat to San Francisco for three days of meetings with Admiral King.

Here for the first time Commander Rochefort began to get some credit for his radio intelligence interception group for their unraveling of the secrets of Japanese military messages. Week by week the radio intelligence team was producing better results as they discovered more elements of the Japanese secret codes. Here at San Francisco, King exhibited a proper appreciation of Rochefort's efforts.

At this meeting the futures of several officers were appraised. Admiral King was a tough commander. President Roosevelt used to say that King shaved with a blowtorch. Admiral Nimitz was much softer and more gentle in his treatment of people. They made a good team then, King very demanding, and Nimitz tending to be protective and understanding of his commanders, but King always finally having the last word.

At this April meeting, Admiral King expressed considerable uneasiness about Frank Jack Fletcher, whom he did not believe to be aggressive enough in his operations or his attitude.

Nimitz, who had known Fletcher for a long time, protected that admiral from King's criticism, and at this point, King let Nimitz have the benefit of the doubt. For as Nimitz said, and King had to agree, a very good man could sometimes find himself in a bad situation, and at this moment Nimitz did not have any too many commanders whom he could trust with a carrier task force.

Privately Nimitz had some serious reservations about King's attitude toward people, for it was well known throughout the fleet that King was a good hater. If he once got down on a man, which he could do for some infringement of discipline or naval courtesy, King neither forgot nor forgave. A number of officers who got on King's bad list suffered from his acerbic personality; their careers were halted in midstream.

At that particular point Admiral Nimitz spoke very highly of Admiral Wilson Brown. He was very pleased with Admiral Brown, following Brown's successful operations in the Lae-Salamaua operation. But King showed a prescience that would serve well in the future. It was all very well about Brown, he said, and Brown had done very well, but Brown was getting on, and pressure was coming from underneath for the younger officers, and particularly the airmen, to be given new and important roles in naval aviation. King, like Fletcher, wore wings but did not pretend to be an airman per se, although he did feel that he had a good sense of the new and coming strategy change that had come about with the development of the carrier. (King's intuition in this regard was not that good. He still stuck by his belief in the battleship fleet, although that fleet had already shown itself too slow and ungainly for carrier operations. King would learn, however, by the experience of the next few weeks.)

There had to be some new assignments of flag officers, which would affect the Pacific Fleet. This matter, brought up at the conference, caused Nimitz considerable worry. He did not want to get involved in personalities, so he and King made an agreement: they would leave the selection of personalities to Admiral Jacobs, the chief of personnel.

The King-Nimitz meetings lasted three days and at the end of them many major changes were forecast for the Pacific Fleet, to come within the next few months. The most important changes would involve the carrier fleet, because it was now apparent that the aircraft carrier was to be the primary weapon of the Pacific war.

Nimitz went back to Pearl Harbor at the end of those meetings to make the best use that he could of his carrier forces.

Chapter 16

The Japanese Plan Goes Askew

During February and March 1942, the American carrier task forces ran the Japanese a merry chase. Halsey and Wilson Brown made several raids. Their task forces, moving around the Central and South Pacific, kept the Japanese off balance and forced several changes in the Japanese expansion plans. The Lae, Salamaua, and Port Moresby operations were originally scheduled for March, then April, and the last was delayed until May by several false stops and starts.

The Japanese won the battle of the Java Sea very handily (as related in *The Triumph of Japan*, Volume I in the Pacific War Series), sinking all the major Allied ships in the Java Sea and putting an end to the American Asiatic fleet. But the American carrier task forces kept moving, and the Japanese kept trying to respond, with no success in coming to grips with the Americans.

In the Dutch East Indies, the remnants of the

Allied expeditionary army forces surrendered at Bandoeng in Java in the second week of March. With that, the American naval command at Pearl Harbor felt that the Japanese would soon begin a move further south. Admiral Brown's successful raid on Lae and Salamaua put a large crimp in that plan, finally bringing about the delay of the Port Moresby operation until May. Admiral Inoue, the commander of the Japanese Fourth Fleet, needed some time to repair ships damaged in these most recent raids.

The setback in the New Guinea campaign also brought Japanese fears that the Americans would continue to make raiding attacks throughout the empire, even unto Japan itself. This fear was brought to fruition with the April delivery by Halsey of the B-25 bombers to the shores of Japan, while one other American task force was cruising in the Coral Sea. At the same time, the Japanese were raiding too, and early in March Nagumo's carrier striking force hit Ceylon, sinking two British cruisers and the old carrier *Hermes*.

In mid-April, Admiral Nimitz sent Admiral Fletcher's Task Force 17 to Tongatabu for supplies. At this point, Nimitz's biggest concern was the Japanese advance southward, which he had orders to contain if possible. At this point the Japanese were intensifying their air attacks on Port Moresby, an almost sure sign that this place would be the target of the next Japanese movement. Nimitz prepared to send Admiral Fletcher's and Admiral Fitch's task forces to contest the Japanese advance. Halsey was not available just then, still being involved in the Tokyo raid, which had not yet come off; he was stealing toward Japan. Thus was developing Phase Two of the Japanese grand strategy, which called for expansion in the South Sea and the ultimate capture of Australia. The original goal of this phase was the consolidation of Japanese defense in the south, for operations against the Allied fleets.

When this was achieved, Japan would then move into the third phase of the plan, which called for the capture of Hawaii and the other American Pacific bases and attacks on the United States, the Panama Canal, and also against Central America, with the purpose of destroying America's will to fight on. At this point, the Japanese hoped, the Americans would be willing to conclude a peace treaty that would enable the Japanese to keep their new empire and complete the conquest of China.

Admiral Yamamoto wanted some changes in that plan, notably the capture of Australia. The army just now balked at this move, on the basis that it would demand far too many army troops and too much army equipment to do the job. Still, Yamamoto was not giving it up. He proposed to extend Japanese fingers into the Solomon Islands chain in the next few months, to be prepared for movement against Australia. Yamamoto wanted to capture Ceylon, too, and Port Darwin in northern Australia, as next steps.

But when the army complained, Yamamoto toned down his demands and settled momentarily for a plan to break up the Allied communications lines between Pearl Harbor and Australia.

The raids on the mandated islands in February and March had given fuel to Yamamoto for his new demands on the navy, that steps be taken to finish the job on the Pacific Fleet with the destruction of the carriers and cruiser forces of that fleet.

Yamamoto was still talking about the "short, decisive war" that he had envisaged from the first. And now he brought Midway into the picture. Midway was the place where he would entice the Americans to fight, defeat them, and then move on to capture Hawaii and make threats against the West Coast of America. The threats would be made by a force that occupied some of the Aleutian islands, and thus pointed a finger at Alaska, Canada, and the Pacific Northwest.

Early in April, Admiral Yamamoto sent emissaries to Tokyo to persuade the Naval General Staff of the sensibility of the Midway operation for the early summer. Once again, as with the Pearl Harbor attack plan, Yamamoto ran into serious opposition, which once again he swept aside with a threat to resign his post as commander of the Combined Fleet if he did not get his way. The navy headquarters was inclined to let Yamamoto have his way once again, particularly on the basis of his success in the first event at Pearl Harbor. But the matter was not entirely settled until Admiral Halsey delivered the B-25 bombers to Tokyo's doorstep. The shock of the bombing of Japan brought even the army around to support of the Midway and Aleutian operations to put an end to the threat of long-range bombing of Tokyo from the Alaskan frontier area, and to put an end to the American carrier raids by the destruction of the American carrier fleet.

The B-25 raid prompted the Japanese to immediate and strong action. A submarine squadron on its way to Truk was diverted and told to go after the Americans. At least two task forces in Japanese waters were getting up steam and ready to give chase. Scores of land-based aircraft were sent out to try to find the American carriers and torpedo them. On the second day, almost every Japanese warship in the home islands was committed to the hunt for the American task force. Admiral Nagumo's big striking force, on the way home from its successful strike against the British fleet off Ceylon, was called to give chase. For two days the whole Japanese fleet establishment was in turmoil until Admiral Yamamoto finally called off the searches as unproductive and too late.

In Tokyo, however, the Doolittle raid produced that most important immediate result: it caused the immediate evaporation of all the opposition from the army and the navy conservatives against the Midway operation and the long-range plan to occupy the Aleutians and perhaps parts of Alaska to prevent any further American air raids on Japan.

Immediately after the Doolittle raid, Admiral

Nimitz turned his attention to the problems of containing the Japanese in the South Pacific, a most difficult job with the limited resources at his command and the great distances involved. He had to take immediate action in the South Pacific, for the operation against Port Moresby, he could tell from radio traffic, was about to begin.

"We are taking steps to oppose Japan's expected move in the Southwest Pacific," Nimitz wrote in his daily war diary. In this Nimitz was backed entirely by Admiral King, who had been asking for stronger Pacific Fleet action for many weeks and was just now about to get it.

On April 20 the operations of the Japanese began to take shape. That day a radio intercept obtained at the reinforced radio intelligence unit at Pearl Harbor indicated that Japanese carriers would be coming into Truk on April 25 to participate in the new operation.

Admiral Nimitz's intelligence indicated that the Japanese movement would aim for the capture of New Guinea.

One of the first moves was to order Admiral Fitch and Admiral Fletcher to combine forces, which put together two fleet carriers to oppose the Japanese. The Australians would contribute their cruiser force to the cause. And General MacArthur's land-based air force in Australia and New Guinea could be counted on to help out.

Because of the American carrier raids in the past three months, the Japanese had become much more cautious in their assessment of the needs of an invasion. Earlier because of the enormous success of their efforts in the early days of the war, without much carrier support, they had been willing to go with little or no carrier support so long as they had land-based airplanes to watch over their ships.

But now, the Tokyo raid had made some changes in Japanese thinking. Admiral Yamamoto insisted on sending at least two carriers from the Striking Force down to the South Pacific to participate in the operations around New Guinea and the Solomons. However, those two carriers were wanted back in May, because the fleet was planning the Midway operation for June. This meant that Admiral Inouye, whose plans had already been knocked askew by the American carrier operations around Rabaul and at Lae and Salamaua, now would have to complete his operations against Port Moresby early in May.

Also Admiral Inouye was waiting for land-based aircraft that had been promised for Rabaul but had not yet appeared. And to add to his troubles came the word that the carrier *Kaga*, which was undergoing some repair, would not be ready in time to participate in the Port Moresby capture. He would get the use of the carriers *Zuikaku* and *Shokaku* but it was not the same. The pilots of *Kaga* and *Akagi* were the best trained in the fleet. Those of *Shokaku* and *Zuikaku* were perhaps half as experienced. And the final shock was that the *Zuikaku* and *Shokaku*, which would support the Port Moresby operation, would also have to support the invasion of Tulagi and establishment of the sea-plane base. Why was the seaplane base necessary, Admiral Inouye wanted to know. Because only with seaplane bases there and at the Deboyne Islands at the northern end of the Coral Sea would the Japanese be able to check to see if American task forces were moving about this area.

Admiral Hara, the commander of Carrier Division Five, also learned that he would be expected first to make a strike on the northern shore of Australia. This additional plan gave him too many things to do, too many chances for disaster, and he appealed to Inouye, complaining that he had too many assigned tasks.

Inouye could not make up his mind exactly what he wanted Hara to do with his carriers, but finally he gave him discretion to drop the Australian raids if necessary. Hara lost no time in scrubbing those from his calendar.

But Hara got another job that he had to undertake: to use his carriers to ferry Zero fighters to Rabaul.

Toward the end of April Washington panicked when a message was deciphered that asked for a thousand copies of maps of northern Australia. ONI Washington immediately leaped to the conclusion that an invasion of Australia was planned to occur in the next few weeks. But at Pearl Harbor, where Commander Rochefort's radio intelligence unit was keeping much better track of the Japanese, it was known that the operations for the next few weeks would be in the Coral Sea area, and not against northern Australia.

This time, Admiral Nimitz's Pearl Harbor command was ready. Both Admiral Fletcher's and Admiral Fitch's carrier task forces had along a radio intelligence unit, which consisted of a Japanese language officer and two or three radiomen whose task was to monitor and read the Japanese radio broadcasts that emanated from the ships in the area. The only problem was that Admiral Fletcher, who was a very old-fashioned man, had not been indoctrinated about the radio intelligence breakthroughs, and he neither trusted the system nor was inclined to listen to the advice of a junior special officer, who was not even a graduate of the naval academy!

Admiral Fletcher had also made the mistake of demanding at a casual luncheon discussion in the wardroom of the *Yorktown* that the young lieutenant on his ship reveal all the workings of the radio intelligence system. Since all this was secret, and most of the admiral's staff at the table had not been cleared, the lieutenant refused to talk. Thus Admiral Fletcher became angry, and because of it, he would refuse to pay any attention to the lieutenant's advice at the critical moment, thus in part at least causing the loss of the carrier *Lexington* and the failure of the Americans to win a clear-cut victory in the coming battle of the Coral Sea.*

*The story of the Battle of the Coral Sea is told in *Stirrings*, Volume 2 of the Pacific War Series.

As the Battle of the Coral Sea turned out, it would be a victory for the Japanese, largely because of Admiral Fletcher's errors, but at the same time it was the first time in the history of the Pacific War that a Japanese military effort had been stopped cold. The Tulagi seaplane base they established was crippled and would be easy prey to the Guadalcanal invasion force a few weeks later, and the attempt to capture Port Moresby was stopped before it really got started and would never be.

Most important about the Coral Sea battle is that the numerically inferior American forces had been led to the right place at the right time by the radio intelligence emanating from Pearl Harbor.

At the same time a fierce battle had been conducted between the radio intelligence offices in Washington, which advised Admiral King, and the office in Pearl Harbor, which advised Admiral Nimitz. In this struggle, the Pearl Harbor radio intelligence unit was proved to be right in its following of Japanese plans, and the Washington office wrong. Admiral King had been following the advice of the Washington office, and had therefore issued a number of wrongheaded orders to Nimitz, which had delayed and confused the American war effort. Fortunately this was resolved in the matter of the Midway operation, well before the Japanese attack, and then for the first time King began to admit that the Pearl Harbor command knew what it was doing. Thereafter, and for the rest of the war, King kept his interference with Admiral Nimitz to a minimum. It had taken a long time, from well before the day of the Pearl Harbor attack until nearly June 1, 1942, for the Pearl Harbor command to be recognized as having the best assessment and being the most competent to deal with the Japanese, but finally it had come about on the eve of the Battle of Midway, just in time, for if the Washington assessments had been followed that June, Midway would have been another Japanese triumph, instead of what it became, which was the turning point of the Pacific naval war.

Notes

1 The Darkening Clouds

The material for chapter 1 comes from various sources consulted in previous books of this series and about Japan, particularly for my *Japan's War* (McGraw-Hill, 1986) and *The Rise of the Chinese Republic* (McGraw-Hill, 1988).

2 Roots of Conflict

Much of the material for this chapter comes from research done for my *Pacific Destiny* (W. W. Norton, 1980). Some of the material comes from research for *The Fall of Tsingtao* (Arthur Barker, London, 1972). The material about Shanghai in the 1930s is from my own experience in China in the 1940s. The material about China and the Burma road comes from my World War II experience in Burma and China. The material about Admiral Yamamoto comes from my researches into the life of Admiral Yamamoto, which culminated in my biography, *Yamamoto* (McGraw-Hill, 1989).

3 War Plans

The material and the quotations from Yamamoto are from his story, and from the diary of Admiral Matome Ugaki, his chief of staff, which was published in Japan but never translated into English.

The statistics about the comparative strengths of the United States and Japanese naval forces come from the Boei Senshi Shitsu (War History Room) history of Japan's war effort, and particularly the volume on Hawaii operations. The material about Admiral Richmond Kelly Turner's experience with the Japanese is from Admiral George Dyer's *The Amphibians Came to Conquer, The Biography of Admiral Turner*, published by the U.S. Navy.

The material about Japanese movements in the 1930s and 1940s is from Morison, and from materials collected for *Japan's War*. The material about the liaison conferences is from the record of the liaison conferences in the Japanese archives.

4 The Japanese Plan

Yamamoto's letters are from his correspondence, some of it in the museum of Nagaoka High School, in Nagaoka (Niigata), Japan. Some of the material about Yamamoto's activities is from the Ugaki diary of the period. Some of the material is from Commander Genda's articles in the *Proceedings of the U.S. Naval Institute* dealing with the Pearl

Harbor operations. Some comes from Prange's *At Dawn We Slept*. The material about the planning for Pearl Harbor is largely from the Boei volume on Pearl Harbor operations.

5 How Ready Can Ready Be?

The material about the readiness quotient of the Americans at Pearl Harbor comes from the Wohlstetter book, from Prange, and from Layton. Layton has traced the entire history of the conflict between Pearl Harbor and Washington over naval intelligence, its dissemination, and its practices. Some of this was also indicated in W. J. Holmes's *Double-Edged Secrets*. The information about Yamamoto's attitude toward carrier warfare is from materials collected for my biography of Yamamoto. Much of the material about Kimmel is from the Cincpac files, and from the Layton book.

The material about the events in Washington in the period is largely from Prange and Layton. The material about Japan in the same period is from my studies for *Japan's War*. The story of the Farthing report is from Layton and Prange.

6 The Attacking Force

Much of the material for this chapter comes from research in Japan done in connection with my biography of Yamamoto. The enmity between Nagumo and Yamamoto went back to the early 1930s when Yamamoto was a strong advocate of the "treaty" faction of the navy and Nagumo was an adherent of the "fleet" faction. The story of Japanese torpedo research comes from the Boei Hawaii volume and from Prange's *At Dawn We Slept*, published by McGraw-Hill. The material about the midget submarines is from the Boei volume on submarine warfare. The discussion of the route of the attack is from Layton. The material about Japanese plans and training is largely from the Ugaki diary. The material about Admiral Nagumo and Admiral Yamamoto is largely from the Ugaki diary, and from Layton. The order of sailing of the ships and the material about preparations comes mostly from the Boei Hawaii operations volume.

7 December 6 — At Sea

The story of the *Taiyo Maru* is from the Layton book. The material about the sailing of the submarines is from Sakamaki and Prange. The account of the tension in Japan is from the Ugaki diary. The material about General Tojo and the Emperor is from research done for my biographies of Tojo and Hirohito. The day-by-day countdown of the last few days is from Layton, Boei Hawaii, and from Prange. Ensign Sakamaki's remarks come from his book *I Attacked Pearl Harbor*.

8 The Problem of Readiness

The material about Admiral Kimmel and General Short comes from the Robertson report and from Layton. Layton's argument that a great wrong had been done by the placement of blame in the wrong places was extremely convincing to me. His accounts of the code-breaking operations and those of W. J. Holmes were used here. The material about Secretary Hull's harsh note and the Japanese reaction to it comes from various written sources, but most impressive to me was a conversation with Ian Mutsu, the son of a Japanese diplomat, whose father had predicted war after he heard of the Hull note. Forty years later, Mutsu recalled clearly his father's shocked reaction to the Hull statements. The material about the day-to-day countdown is from Layton. The notes about the *Ward* are from Commander Outerbridge's narrative in the Navy Department files.

9 Attack!

The Outerbridge story comes from his combat narrative. The story of the Japanese striking force comes from Prange and from the Boei Hawaii volume. The material about General Marshall is from the Layton book. The material about the Opana tracking station is from Prange.

10 The First Wave

The material about the encounters with Japanese submarines is from Morison and from

Outerbridge. The story of Commander Fuchida is from the Boei Hawaii operations book. The material about Admiral Yamamoto is from the Ugaki diary. The story of the air strike is from the Hawaii volume and from Prange. The story of Lt. Bonnell is from his combat narrative in the navy files. The story of Lt. Kaminski's troubles is from Layton. Admiral Furlong's story comes from Morison. The unfolding story of the defenders in the Pearl Harbor attack is largely from Layton.

11 The Attack Continues

The story of the destroyers is from Outerbridge and Morison. The account of the events in Washington is from Layton and Morison. The accounts of the B-17s come from Prange and Morison. The story of the ships in the harbor is from Morison and the Cincpac records. The account of events at fleet headquarters is from Layton. The stories of Lieutenants Welch and Taylor are from Prange. The account of the second Japanese attack is from the Boei Hawaii book. The events in the harbor here were described by Morison.

12 Admiral Nagumo

The story of Admiral Nagumo's actions and conversations is from the Boei history and from Prange. The accounts of events in Manila come from papers in the MacArthur Memorial Museum in Norfolk, Virginia, where some of the rec-

261

ords of the USAFFE command can be found. General Brereton's activities were reported in his command's war diary here. The account of Fuchida's activity is from Prange. The account of the discussions between Genda and Nagumo is also from the Prange book. Admiral Ugaki's reactions are given in his diary.

13 Aftermath at Pearl

The reactions of Hawaii to the attack can be found in the pages of the *Honolulu Star Bulletin* and the *Honolulu Advertiser* for the period. The account of events at the Japanese consulate is from Prange. The story of reactions in Washington is from Morison and Layton. The account of the activity of the destroyers is from the Outerbridge narrative. The account of the defense of Wake is from Morison. The material about the Cincpac command comes from the Cincpac records in the Navy Department and from Layton.

The account of events at Pearl Harbor on the second day is from the Cincpac records. The Kuroshima story is partly from the Ugaki diary and partly from Prange. The material about ONI is from Layton. The story of the Japanese withdrawal is from the Boei Hawaii operations book. The story of Admiral Yamamoto's activities and his attitudes is from Ugaki.

The plans of Admiral Kimmel come from the Cincpac records. The story of the Knox trip is told in Knox's narrative in the Library of Congress and in the Knox report. The interaction between Knox and Kimmel is related in Layton and Prange.

14 More Confusion

The story of the Nagumo trip home to Japan is from the Boei Hawaii volume and from Layton. The material about Kimmel and Stark is from Morison and Layton. The material about the changeover of command is from the records of Cincpac and materials gathered for *Nimitz and His Admirals, How They Won the War in the Pacific*, Weybright and Talley, 1970.

The story of the abortive Wake Island relief expedition is from the Cincpac records and from Layton. The Pye-Stark interaction is from Morison. The account of the defense of Wake is from Layton and Morison and the Cincpac records. The discussion of the attitudes of the admirals comes from a long conversation the author had with Admiral Fitch. The story of the Roberts Commission investigation is largely from Layton.

15 The Fleet Fights

The situation at Cincpac headquarters after the Pearl Harbor attack is discussed by Layton. The coming of Nimitz is from his letters to his wife and from the Cincpac records. The story of Halsey's various attacks on Japanese outposts in the early months of 1942 is from Cincpac records and the records of Halsey's task force. The story of Admiral Brown's raid on New Guinea is from the records of his task force in the Cincpac files.

The material about Admiral Towers and the young aviators is from conversations with Admiral Hill, Mrs. John Towers, Admiral Hoover, and others. The story of the King-Nimitz meeting of April 1942 is from the record of the King-Nimitz meetings.

16 The Japanese Plan Goes Askew

The stories of the activities of the American task forces are from the Cincpac records and from Layton and Morison. The details of the Yamamoto plan are from materials assembled for my biography of Admiral Yamamoto. The story of the Japanese and American activities on the eve of the battle of the Coral Sea is from Morison and the Cincpac records and from Layton.

Bibliography

The basic source for this book about Pearl Harbor was the files of Cincpac in the Operational Archives of the Navy History Center at the Washington Navy Yard. This includes the Cincpac War Diary, the correspondence of Admiral Nimitz, the Wilson Brown papers, the Cincpac Gray Book, the papers of Admiral Towers, and the Towers diaries, Admiral Nimitz's correspondence with Mrs. Nimitz, the fourteenth Naval District War Diary for December 1941, conversations with Admiral Harry W. Hill, Admiral Aubrey Fitch, Admiral Milo F. Draemel, the papers of Secretary Frank Knox, the war diaries of Task Force 8, Task Force 11, and Task Force 17, and combat narratives by Lieutenant Graham C. Bonnell and Commander William W. Outerbridge, the oral history of Admiral C. J. Moore, and the oral history of Admiral Raymond Spruance and Admiral Harry W. Hill.

Published Sources

Hoehling, A. A. *The Week before Pearl Harbor.* New York: W. W. Norton, 1963.

Japanese Defense Agency. Hawaii Operations (in Japanese). Tokyo: Japanese Defense Agency War History Room, 1970.

Layton, Edwin C. *And I Was There . . .* New York: William Morrow, 1985.

Millis, Walter. *This Is Pearl.* Westport, Conn.: Greenwood Press, 1947.

Morison, Samuel Eliot. *The Rising Sun in the Pacific.* Boston: Atlantic Little Brown, 1984.

Prange, Gordon, et al. *December 7, 1941.* New York: McGraw-Hill, 1988.

———. *At Dawn We Slept.* New York: McGraw-Hill, 1981.

Sakamaki, Kazuo. *I Attacked Pearl Harbor.* New York: Association Press, 1949.

Trefousse, Hans Louis. *What Happened at Pearl Harbor.* New York: Twayne Publishers, 1958.

Wohlstetter, Roberta. *Pearl Harbor, Warning and Decision.* Stanford: Stanford University Press, 1962.